MACHINE

LEARNING

© Globaltech NTC

PYTHON MACHINE LEARNING

Machine Learning and Deep Learning with Python, scikit-learn, and TensorFlow

Step-by-Step Tutorial for Beginners

Samuel Burns

contained within this document, including, but not limited to, errors, omissions, or inaccuracies.

Thank you!

Thank you for buying this book! It is intended to help you understanding Machine Learning and Deep learning with Python.

Book Objectives:

The Aims and Objectives of the Book:

- To help you understand the basics of machine learning and deep learning.
- Understand the various categories of machine learning algorithms.
- To help you understand how different machine learning algorithms work.
- You will learn how to implement various machine learning algorithms programmatically in Python.
- To help you learn how to use Scikit-Learn and TensorFlow Libraries in Python.
- To help you know how to analyze data programmatically to extract patterns, trends, and relationships between variables.

What do you need for this Book?

You are required to have installed the following on your computer:

- Python 3.X
- Numpy
- Pandas
- Matplotlib

The Author guides you on how to install the rest of the Python libraries that are required for machine learning and deep learning.

Who this Book is for?

Here are the target readers for this book:

- Anybody who is a complete beginner to machine learning in Python.

- Anybody who needs to advance their programming skills in Python for machine learning programming and deep learning.
- Professionals in data science.
- Professors, lecturers or tutors who are looking to find better ways to explain machine learning to their students in the simplest and easiest way.
- Students and academicians, especially those focusing on neural networks, machine learning, and deep learning.

Why this Book is suitable for you?

If you want to learn machine learning and deep learning with Python, this is the best book for you.
Here are the reasons:
- The author has explored everything about machine learning and deep learning right from the basics.
- A simple language has been used.
- Many examples have been given, both theoretically and programmatically.
- Screenshots showing program outputs have been added.

The book is written chronologically, in a step-by-step manner.

About the Author:

Samuel Burns is Director of Data Science, Cloud and AI, at GlobalTech NTC Belgium. He has a Ph.D. in Machine Learning and is an Artificial Intelligence developer, researcher, and educator as well as an Open Source Software developer. He has authored many papers as well as a number of popular software packages.

From 2008 to 2016 he was Principal Computer Scientist for Data Mining with Nemesis Analytics Sweden. He has served as an Expert and Visiting Professor of the Belgium Academy of Sciences. Specialist in Data Mining and Security, Burns is an active machine learning researcher and regularly teaches courses and maintains resources for the data scientist.

Burn's research has pioneered developments in ensemble learning, outlier detection and profile discovery. He is involved in numerous international artificial intelligence and data mining research activities and conferences.

"Artificial intelligence would be the ultimate version of Google. The ultimate search engine that would understand everything on the web. It would understand exactly what you wanted, and it would give you the right thing. We're nowhere near doing that now. However, we can get incrementally closer to that, and that is basically what we work on."

Larry Page

Introduction

Human beings are known to learn from their experiences. Consider a situation in which you are learning to read or speak a new language. You will show an improvement with time. Machine learning was borrowed from the concept of learning exhibited by human beings. When computer systems are exposed to the same situation repeatedly, they can show an improvement in the way they respond to that situation with time. Machine learning typically relies on data. It involves the design and development of computer systems that can extract patterns, trends, and relationships between various variables in a dataset. Such knowledge can then be used to predict what will happen in the future.

The increasing popularity of machine learning can be attributed to the same factors that are leading to an increased popularity of data mining. For instance, the amount of data available for machine learning increases every day. Data storage costs are going down each day. Cheaper and powerful forms of processing are discovered each day. This book is an exploration of machine learning and deep learning in detail. You will learn how to use Scikit-Learn and TensorFlow libraries in Python for machine learning tasks. Enjoy reading!

Table of Contents

Chapter 1- Getting Started

What is Machine Learning?

Machine learning is a branch of artificial intelligence that provides systems with the ability to learn from experience without being programmed explicitly. Machine learning is concerned with the development of computer applications that can access data and learn from it on themselves.

The learning process begins with data or observations, like instruction, direct experience or examples to extract patterns from the data and use these patterns to make predictions in the future. The primary goal of machine learning is to allow computers to learn automatically without intervention by humans and adjust accordingly.

With machine learning, we can analyze large quantities of data. Machine learning gives us profitable results but we may need a number of resources to reach this point. Additional time may be needed to train the machine learning models.

Classification of Machine Learning Algorithms

The Machine Learning algorithms can fall either in the supervised or unsupervised or reinforced learning.

Supervised Learning

For the case of supervised learning, the human is expected to provide both the inputs and the outputs which are desired and furnish the feedback based on the accuracy of the predictions during training. After completion of the training, the algorithm will have to apply what was applied to the next data.

The concept of supervised learning can be seen to be similar to learning under a teacher's supervision in human beings. The teacher gives some examples to the student, and the student then derives new rules and knowledge from these examples so as to apply this somewhere else.

It is also good for you to know the difference between the regression problems and classification problems. In regression problems, the target is a numeric value, while in classification; the target is a class or a tag. A regression task can help determine the average cost of all houses in London, while a classification task will help determine the types of flowers based on the length of their sepals and petals.

Unsupervised Learning

For the case of unsupervised learning, the algorithms do not expect to be provided with the output data. An approach called deep learning, which is an iterative approach, is used so as to review the data and arrive at new conclusions. This makes them suitable for use in processing tasks which are complex compared to the supervised learning algorithms. This means that the unsupervised learning algorithms learn solely from examples without responses to these. The algorithm finds patterns from the examples on its own.

Supervised learning algorithms work similarly to how humans determine any similarities between two or more objects. Majority of recommender systems you encounter when purchasing items online work based on unsupervised learning algorithms. In this case, the algorithm derives what to suggest to you for purchase from what you have purchased before. The algorithm has to estimate the kind of customers whom you resemble, and a suggestion is drawn from that.

Reinforcement Learning

This type of learning occurs when the algorithm is presented with examples which lack labels, as it is the case with unsupervised learning. However, the example can be accompanied by a positive or a negative feedback depending on the solution which is proposed by the algorithm. It is associated with applications in which the algorithm has to make decisions, and these decisions are associated with a consequence. It is similar to trial and error in human learning.

Errors become useful in learning when they are associated with a penalty such as pain, cost, loss of time etc. In reinforced learning, some actions are more likely to succeed compared to others.

Machine learning processes are similar to those of data mining and predictive modeling. In both cases, searching through the data is required so as to draw patterns then adjust the actions of the program accordingly. A good example of machine learning is the recommender systems. If you purchase an item online, you will get an ad which is related to that item, and that is a good example of machine learning.

What is Deep Learning?

Deep learning is a subfield of machine learning involving algorithms that are inspired by the function and structure of the brain known as artificial neural networks. It teaches computers to do what is natural to humans, that is, learn by example. It is the technology behind the concept of the driverless car.

It is through deep learning that a computer is able to learn to perform classification tasks directly from text, images or sound. Deep learning models are able to achieve a state-of-the-art accuracy, which in some cases exceeds human-level performance. Large sets of labelled data and neural network architectures are used to train models in deep learning.

What is Scikit-Learn?

Scikit-learn provide its users with a number of supervised and unsupervised learning algorithms through a consistent Python interface. It was initially developed by David Cournapeau in 2007 as a Google Summer of code project. Scikit-learn are suitable for both academic and commercial use.

Scikit-learn has been in use as a machine learning library in Python. It comes with numerous classification, regression and clustering algorithms including gradient boosting, and support vector machines (SVMs), random forests, k-means, and DBSCAN. Scikit-learn was designed to be used with other Python libraries including Numpy and SciPy.

The library itself was written in Python and some of its algorithms were written in Cython to offer a better performance. Scikit-learn is a good library for building machine learning models. The library is open source and it is under BSD license.

What is TensorFlow?

TensorFlow is a framework from Google used for the creation of deep learning models. TensorFlow relies on data-flow graphs for numerical computation. TensorFlow has made machine learning easy. It makes the processes of acquiring data, training machine learning models, making predictions and modifying future results easy.

The library was developed by Google's Brain team for use in large-scale machine learning. TensorFlow brings together machine learning and deep learning algorithms and models and it makes them much useful via a common metaphor. TensorFlow uses Python to give its users a front-end API that can be used for building applications, with the applications being executed in high-performance C++.

TensorFlow can be used for building, training and running deep neural networks for image recognition, handwritten digit classification, recurrent neural networks, word embedding, natural language processing etc.

Chapter 2- Environment Setup

Before getting into the practical part of machine learning and deep learning, we need to install our two libraries, that is, Scikit-Learn and TensorFlow.

Installing Scikit-Learn

Scikit-learn is supported in Python 2.7 and above. Before installing Scikit-learn, ensure that you have Numpy and SciPy libraries already installed. Also, ensure that you have the latest versions of these libraries. Once you have installed these, you can go ahead to install Scikit-learn on your machine.

The installation of these libraries can be done using pip. Pip is a tool that comes with Python, meaning after installing Python, you get pip. To install scikit-learn, run the following command on the terminal of your operating system:

pip install scikit-learn

The installation should run and come to a completion.

You can also use conda to install scikit-learn. This can be done by running the following command:

conda install scikit-learn

Once the installation of sckit-learn is complete, you need to import it into your Python program in order to use its algorithms. This can be done by using the *import* statement as shown below:

import sklearn

If the command runs without an error, know that the installation of scikit-learn was successful. If the command generates an error, note that the installation was not successful.

You can now use scikit-learn to create your own machine learning models.

Installing TensorFlow

TensorFlow comes with APIs for programming languages like C++, Haskell, Go, Java, Rust, and it comes with a third-party package for R known as *tensorflow*. We will be guiding you on how to install TensorFlow on Windows. On Windows, TensorFlow can be installed with pip or Anaconda.

The native pip will install the TensorFlow on your system without having to go through a virtual environment. However, note that the installation of TensorFlow with pip may interfere with other Python installations on your system. However, the good thing is that you only have to run a single command and TensorFlow will be installed on your system. Also, when TensorFlow is installed via pip, users will be allowed to run the TensorFlow programs from the directory they want.

To install TensorFlow with Anaconda, you may have to create a virtual environment. However, within the Anaconda itself, it is recommended that you install TensorFlow via the *pip install* command rather than the *conda install* command.

Ensure that you have installed Python 3.5 and above on your Windows system. Python3 comes with a pip3 program which can be used for installation of TensorFlow. This means we should use the *pip3 install* command for installation purposes. The following command will help you install CPU-only version for TensorFlow:

pip3 install --upgrade tensorflow

The command should be run from the command line:

```
C:\Windows\system32>
C:\Windows\system32>pip3 install --upgrade tensorflow
Collecting tensorflow
  Downloading https://files.pythonhosted.org/packages/af/5b/695e2e66feb27742a78f
938d8369cc874b5fc7082193c3352c9db599af01/tensorflow-1.11.0-cp35-cp35m-win_amd64.
whl (46.9MB)
    22% |#######                         | 10.4MB 273kB/s eta 0:02:14
```

If you need to install a GPU version for TensorFlow, run this command:

pip3 install --upgrade tensorflow-gpu

This will install TensorFlow on your Windows system.

You can also install TensorFlow with the Anaconda package. Pip comes installed with Python, but Anaconda doesn't. This means that to install TensorFlow with Anaconda, you should first install the Anaconda. You can download Anaconda from its website and find the installation instructions from the same site.

Once you install Anaconda, you get a package named *conda,* which is good for the management of virtual environments and the installation of packages. To get to use this package, you should start the Anaconda.

On Windows, click Start, choose "All Programs", expand the "Anaconda ..." folder then click the "Anaconda Prompt". This should launch the anaconda prompt on your system. If you need to see the details of the conda package. Just run the following command on the terminal you have just opened:

conda info

This should return more details regarding the package manager.

```
(tensorenviron) C:\Users\admin\Documents>conda info
Current conda install:

               platform : win-64
          conda version : 4.3.27
       conda is private : False
      conda-env version : 4.3.27
    conda-build version : 3.0.22
         python version : 3.6.2.final.0
       requests version : 2.18.4
       root environment : C:\Users\admin\Anaconda3  (writable)
    default environment : C:\Users\admin\Anaconda3\envs\tensorenviron
       envs directories : C:\Users\admin\Anaconda3\envs
                          C:\Users\admin\AppData\Local\conda\conda\envs
                          C:\Users\admin\.conda\envs
          package cache : C:\Users\admin\Anaconda3\pkgs
                          C:\Users\admin\AppData\Local\conda\conda\pkgs
            channel URLs : https://repo.continuum.io/pkgs/main/win-64
                          https://repo.continuum.io/pkgs/main/noarch
                          https://repo.continuum.io/pkgs/free/win-64
                          https://repo.continuum.io/pkgs/free/noarch
                          https://repo.continuum.io/pkgs/r/win-64
                          https://repo.continuum.io/pkgs/r/noarch
                          https://repo.continuum.io/pkgs/pro/win-64
                          https://repo.continuum.io/pkgs/pro/noarch
                          https://repo.continuum.io/pkgs/msys2/win-64
                          https://repo.continuum.io/pkgs/msys2/noarch
            config file : None
             netrc file : None
           offline mode : False
             user-agent : conda/4.3.27 requests/2.18.4 CPython/3.6.2 Windows/7 W
indows/6.1.7601
          administrator : False

(tensorenviron) C:\Users\admin\Documents>
```

There is something unique with Anaconda. It helps us create a virtual Python environment using the conda package. This virtual environment is simply an isolated copy of Python with the capability of maintaining its own files, paths, and directories so that you may be able to work with specific versions of Python or other libraries without affecting your other Python projects. Virtual environments provide us with a way of isolating projects and avoid problems that may arise as a result of version requirements and different dependencies across various components. Note that this virtual environment will remain separate from your normal Python environment meaning that the packages installed in the virtual environment will not affect the ones you have in your Python's normal environment.

We need to create a virtual environment for the TensorFlow package. This can be done via the *conda create* command. The command takes the syntax given below:

conda create -n [environment-name]

In our case, we need to give this environment the name *tensorenviron.* We can create it by running the following command:

conda create -n tensorenviron

You will be asked whether to allow the process of creating the environment to continue or not. Type "y" and hit the enter key on the keyboard. The installation will continue successfully.

```
(C:\Users\admin\Anaconda3) C:\Users\admin\Documents>conda create -n tensorenviro
n
Fetching package metadata ............
Solving package specifications:
Package plan for installation in environment C:\Users\admin\Anaconda3\envs\tenso
renviron:

Proceed ([y]/n)?

#
# To activate this environment, use:
# > activate tensorenviron
#
# To deactivate an active environment, use:
# > deactivate
#
# * for power-users using bash, you must source
#
```

After creating an environment, we should activate it so that we may be able to use it. The activation can be done using the *activate* command followed by the name of the environment as shown below:

activate tensorenviron

Now that you have activated the TensorFlow environment, you can go ahead and install TensorFlow package in it. You can achieve this by running the following command:

conda install tensorflow

You will be presented with a list of packages that will be installed together with the TensorFlow package. You will be prompted to permit the installation of these packages. Just type "y" then hit the enter key on your keyboard. The installation of the packages will begin immediately. Note that the installation process may take a number of minutes, so remain patient. However, the speed of your internet connection will determine how long this process takes. The progress of the installation process will also be shown on the prompt window.

```
(tensorenviron) C:\Users\admin\Documents>conda install tensorflow
Fetching package metadata .............
Solving package specifications: .

Package plan for installation in environment C:\Users\admin\Anaconda3\envs\tenso
renviron:

The following NEW packages will be INSTALLED:

    _tflow_select:       2.1.0-gpu
    absl-py:             0.6.1-py36_0
    astor:               0.7.1-py36_0
    blas:                1.0-mkl
    certifi:             2018.10.15-py36_0
    cudatoolkit:         9.0-1
    cudnn:               7.1.4-cuda9.0_0
    gast:                0.2.0-py36_0
    grpcio:              1.12.1-py36h1a1b453_0
    h5py:                2.8.0-py36h3bdd7fb_2
    hdf5:                1.10.2-hac2f561_1
    icc_rt:              2017.0.4-h97af966_0
    intel-openmp:        2019.0-118
    keras-applications:  1.0.6-py36_0
    keras-preprocessing: 1.0.5-py36_0
    libprotobuf:         3.6.1-h7bd577a_0
    markdown:            3.0.1-py36_0
    mkl:                 2019.0-118
    mkl_fft:             1.0.6-py36hdbbee80_0
    mkl_random:          1.0.1-py36h77b88f5_1
    numpy:               1.15.3-py36ha559c80_0
    numpy-base:          1.15.3-py36h8128ebf_0
    pip:                 10.0.1-py36_0
    protobuf:            3.6.1-py36h33f27b4_0
    python:              3.6.7-h33f27b4_1
    scipy:               1.1.0-py36h4f6bf74_1
    setuptools:          40.5.0-py36_0
    six:                 1.11.0-py36_1
    tensorboard:         1.11.0-py36he025d50_0
    tensorflow:          1.11.0-gpu_py36h5dc63e2_0
    tensorflow-base:     1.11.0-gpu_py36h6e53903_0
    termcolor:           1.1.0-py36_1
    vc:                  14.1-h0510ff6_4
    vs2015_runtime:      14.15.26706-h3a45250_0
    werkzeug:            0.14.1-py36_0
    wheel:               0.32.2-py36_0
    wincertstore:        0.2-py36h7fe50ca_0
    zlib:                1.2.11-h8395fce_2

Proceed ([y]/n)? y

_tflow_select- 100%  |###############################| Time: 0:00:00 598.96 kB/s
blas-1.0-mkl.t 100%  |###############################| Time: 0:00:00 475.58 kB/s
cudatoolkit-9. 100%  |###############################| Time: 0:21:50 271.86 kB/s
intel-openmp-2 100%  |###############################| Time: 0:00:06 274.72 kB/s
vs2015_runtime 100%  |###############################| Time: 0:00:08 275.83 kB/s
cudnn-7.1.4-cu 100%  |###############################| Time: 0:12:12 275.45 kB/s
```

After some time, the installation process will complete and it is time for you to verify whether the installation was successful. We can simply do this by running the Python's *import* statement. The statement should be run from the Python's terminal. While on the Anaconda prompt, type *python* and hit the enter key. This should take you to the Python terminal. Now run the following *import* statement:

import tensorflow as tf

If the package was not installed successful, you will get an error, otherwise, the installation of the package was successful.

Chapter 3- Using Scikit-Learn

Now that you are done with the installations, you can begin to use the libraries. We will begin with the Scikit-Learn library.

To be able to use scikit-learn in your code, you should first import it by running this statement:

import sklearn

Loading Datasets

Machine learning is all about analyzing sets of data. Before this, we should first load the dataset into our workspace. The library comes loaded with a number of datasets that we can load and work with. We will demonstrate this by using a dataset known as *Iris*. This is a dataset of flowers. The following code shows how we can use scikit-learn to load the dataset:

```
# Import scikit-learn library
from sklearn import datasets
# Load iris dataset
iris= datasets.load_iris()
# Confirm by printing the shape of the data
print(iris.data.shape)
```

The code returns the following:

```
(150, 4)
```

The above output shows that the dataset has 150 rows and 4 columns. To print the whole data on the Python terminal, run the following statement:

```
print(iris.data)

[[ 5.1  3.5  1.4  0.2]
 [ 4.9  3.   1.4  0.2]
 [ 4.7  3.2  1.3  0.2]
 [ 4.6  3.1  1.5  0.2]
 [ 5.   3.6  1.4  0.2]
 [ 5.4  3.9  1.7  0.4]
 [ 4.6  3.4  1.4  0.3]
 [ 5.   3.4  1.5  0.2]
 [ 4.4  2.9  1.4  0.2]
 [ 4.9  3.1  1.5  0.1]
 [ 5.4  3.7  1.5  0.2]
 [ 4.8  3.4  1.6  0.2]
 [ 4.8  3.   1.4  0.1]
 [ 4.3  3.   1.1  0.1]
 [ 5.8  4.   1.2  0.2]
 [ 5.7  4.4  1.5  0.4]
 [ 5.4  3.9  1.3  0.4]
 [ 5.1  3.5  1.4  0.3]
 [ 5.7  3.8  1.7  0.3]
 [ 5.1  3.8  1.5  0.3]
 [ 5.4  3.4  1.7  0.2]
 [ 5.1  3.7  1.5  0.4]
 [ 4.6  3.6  1.   0.2]
 [ 5.1  3.3  1.7  0.5]
 [ 4.8  3.4  1.9  0.2]
 [ 5.   3.   1.6  0.2]
 [ 5.   3.4  1.6  0.4]
 [ 5.2  3.5  1.5  0.2]
 [ 5.2  3.4  1.4  0.2]
 [ 4.7  3.2  1.6  0.2]
 [ 4.8  3.1  1.6  0.2]
```

Chapter 4- Linear Regression with Scikit-Learn

We need to discuss Linear Regression in details and see how we can implement it with the scikit-learn library.

In Linear Algebra, the term "linearity" is used to denote the relationship between two or even more variables. If this relationship is represented in a two dimensional space, we end up with a straight line.

Consider a case in which we need to determine a linear relationship between the number of hours a student spends studying for a test and the percentage of marks the student scores in the test. We need to be able to tell the percentage of marks that a student can score if we are given the number of hours the student spent preparing for the test. If the independent variable (hours) is plotted on the x-axis while the dependent variable (percentage) is plotted on the y-axis, linear regression will give a straight line representing the best fit for the points.

The equation of a straight line is given by the following formula:

```
y = mx + b
```

In the above equation, m denotes the slope of the line while b denotes the intercept. This means that the linear regression algorithm gives us the most optimal values for the slope and the intercept. The variables x and y will remain the same as they are data features that cannot be changed. We can get many different lines depending on the values of slope and the intercept that we use. Basically, a linear regression algorithm works by fitting multiple lines on data points and returns the line with the least error.

The same can be extended in cases where we have more than two variables. This is referred to as *multiple linear regression.* In such a case,

37

we have many independent variables upon which the dependent variable relies. A good example is when you need to predict the price of land based on factors the size of the land, the type of soil, the location of the land, the average income of the individuals in that area etc. The dependent price (price) depends on many independent variables. A regression model with multiple variables can be represented as follows:

```
y = b0 + m1b1 + m2b2 + m3b3 + ... mnbn
```

The above formula is an equation for a hyper plane.

Now that you are conversant with the concept of Linear Regression, let us see how we can implement Linear Regression functions in the Scikit-Learn library. We will begin with a simple linear regression involving two variables then proceed to a multiple linear regression involving many variables.

Simple Linear Regression

We need to use our previous example, which is, predicting the number of marks a student will score in a test depending on the number of hours they have studied for the test. It is a simple linear regression task since we only have two variables.

Import Libraries

Run the following Python statements tom import all the necessary libraries:

```
import numpy as np
import pandas as pd
```

import matplotlib.pyplot as plt

I have the dataset saved in an MS Excel file named *student_marks.csv*. I have kept this file in the directory where I save my Python scripts, so I will not have to give the path leading to the file. The .csv extension in the filename shows that it is a comma separate values file.

You can download the file *student_marks.csv* here: https://ufile.io/vblmj

The following statement will help us to import the dataset into the workspace. We are using the Pandas library (we imported it as *pd*) for this:

dataset = pd.read_csv('student_marks.csv')

We can now explore the dataset to know more about it and see what it has. Go directly to the Python terminal and type this:

dataset.shape

Which returns the following:

```
>>> dataset.shape

(25, 2)
>>>
```

Which means that the dataset has 25 rows and 2 columns.

To see the first five rows of the data, call *head()* function as follows:

dataset.head()

```
>>> dataset.head()
    Hours    Marks
0     2.5      21
1     5.1      47
2     3.2      27
3     8.5      75
4     3.5      30
>>>
```

However, you may get an error when you attempt to print the data as shown above. The cause of the error could be that Pandas is looking for the amount of information to display, so you should provide sys output information.

The error can be solved by modifying your code to the following:

```
import numpy as np
import pandas as pd
import matplotlib.pyplot as plt
import sys
sys.__stdout__  = sys.stdout
dataset = pd.read_csv('student_marks.csv')
print(dataset.head())
```

We have simply provided the information to the *sys* library.

To see the statistical details of the dataset, we call the *describe()* function as follows:

dataset.describe()

```
>>> dataset.describe()
           Hours       Marks
count   25.000000   25.000000
mean     5.012000   51.480000
std      2.525094   25.286887
min      1.100000   17.000000
25%      2.700000   30.000000
50%      4.800000   47.000000
75%      7.400000   75.000000
max      9.200000   95.000000
>>> |
```

We can now plot the data points on a 2-D graph and see how they are distributed. You no appreciate why we imported the *Matplotlib* library. The following code will help you to plot the datapoints:

```
dataset.plot(x='Hours', y='Marks', style='o')
plt.title('Hours vs Marks(%)')
plt.xlabel('Hours')
plt.ylabel('Marks (%)')
plt.show()
```

The code returns the following plot:

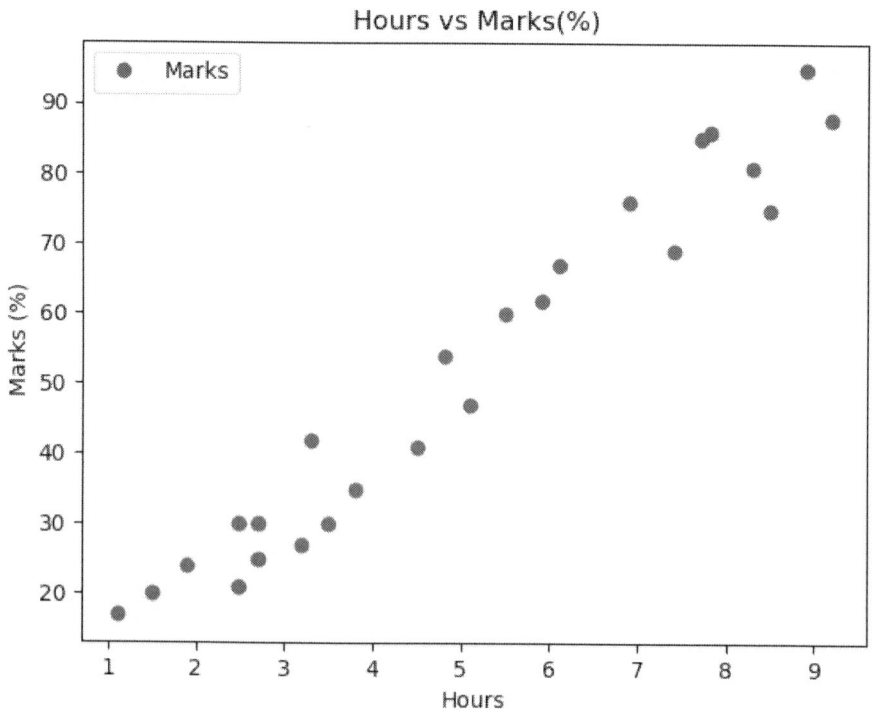

Hours vs Marks(%)

We have called the *plot()* function provided by the Pandas library. We passed the column names to this function and it was able to create and display the plot. The *show()* function helped us to display the plot.

Data Preparation

Preparation of the data should involve subdividing it into *attributes* and *labels*. Attributes should form the independent variables while labels should form the dependent variables whose values we need to predict. Our dataset has only two columns. We are predicting Marks based on Hours. This means Hours will form the attribute while Marks will form the label. The attributes and labels can be extracted by running the following code:

```
X = dataset.iloc[:, :-1].values
y = dataset.iloc[:, 1].values
```

The X variable will store the attributes. Note that we have used -1 because we need all columns to be assigned to attributes except the last one, that is, Marks. The y variable will store the labels. Here, we have used 1 since the column for Marks is at index 1. Remember that column indexes begin at index 0.

At this point, we have the attributes and labels for the dataset. We need to divide our data into two sets, namely the *training* and *test* sets. The Scikit-Learn library provides us with a method named "train_test_split()" which can be used for this. It can be used as shown below:

First, import the above method from Scikit-Learn:

from sklearn.model_selection import train_test_split

Now run the following statement:

```
X_train, X_test, y_train, y_test =
train_test_split(X, y, test_size=0.2,
random_state=0)
```

Notice the use of 0.2 for the *test_size* parameter. This means that 20% of the data will be used as the test set while the remaining 80% will be used as the training set.

Training the Algorithm

We will be training the algorithm using the *LinearRegression* class which must be imported from Scikit-Learn. The import can be done as follows;

from sklearn.linear_model import LinearRegression

Now that we have imported the class, we need to instantiate it and give the instance the name *linear_regressor*. This is demonstrated below:

linear_regressor = LinearRegression()

Let us now call the *fit()* method and pass the training data to it:

linear_regressor.fit(X_train, y_train)

As we had stated earlier, Linear Regression works by finding the best values for the slope and the intercept. This is what we have done above. These two have been calculated, so we only have to view their values.

To see the intercept, run the following command:

print(linear_regressor.intercept_)

This returns the following:

```
>>> print(linear_regressor.intercept_)

2.01816004143
>>>
```

We can now view the value of the slope by running the following command:

```
>>> print(linear_regressor.coef_)

[ 9.91065648]
>>>
```

This means that if the student studies an extra hour, they will increase their marks by 9.91%.

Predicting

In the training done above, we have created a linear regression model, which is the equation. The values for the slope and the intercept are known. We can make predictions based on the data we preserved as the training set. The following statement helps us make predictions from the test data:

pred_y = linear_regressor.predict(X_test)

We have simply created a numpy array named *predict_y*. This will have all the predicted values for y from the input values contained in the *X_test* series.

We now have the actual values for the X_test as well as the predicted values. We need to compare between these two and see the amount of similarity or difference between the two. Just run the following code:

```
df = pd.DataFrame({'Actual': y_test,
'Predicted': pred_y})
print(df)
```

It returns the following results:

The model is not accurate, but the values are close to each other.

Evaluating the Accuracy

We now need to evaluate the accuracy of our algorithm. We need to determine how well the algorithm performed on the dataset. When it comes to regression algorithms, three evaluation metrics are used. These include the following:

1. MAE (Mean Absolute Error) - this is the mean of the absolute value of the errors.

2. MSE (Mean Square Error) - this is the mean of squared errors.

3. RMSE (Root Mean Squared Error) - this is the square root of the mean of the squared errors.

The good thing is that we are not required to calculate these manually. The Scikit-Learn library provides us with a number of functions that can be used for this.

We will use the test data to determine the values for these metrics. First, import the *metrics* class from Scikit-Learn:

from sklearn import metrics

Now, run the following command to do the calculation:

```
print('MAE:',
metrics.mean_absolute_error(y_test, pred_y))
print('MSE:', metrics.mean_squared_error(y_test,
pred_y))
print('RMSE:',
np.sqrt(metrics.mean_squared_error(y_test,
pred_y)))
```

The code returns the following values:

```
MAE: 4.183859899
MSE: 21.5987693072
RMSE: 4.6474476121
```

The value for root mean squared error is 4.65. This is less than 10% of mean value of percentages of all students, which are 51.48. Conclusion, our algorithm did a commendable job.

Here is the full code that should give you the values for the errors:

```
import numpy as np
import pandas as pd
import matplotlib.pyplot as plt
```

```
import sys
from sklearn import metrics
from sklearn.model_selection import
train_test_split
from sklearn.linear_model import
LinearRegression
sys.__stdout__ = sys.stdout
dataset = pd.read_csv('student_marks.csv')
X = dataset.iloc[:, :-1].values
y = dataset.iloc[:, 1].values
X_train, X_test, y_train, y_test =
train_test_split(X, y, test_size=0.2,
random_state=0)
linear_regressor = LinearRegression()
linear_regressor.fit(X_train, y_train)
pred_y = linear_regressor.predict(X_test)
df = pd.DataFrame({'Actual': y_test,
'Predicted': pred_y})
print('MAE:',
metrics.mean_absolute_error(y_test, pred_y))
print('MSE:', metrics.mean_squared_error(y_test,
pred_y))
print('RMSE:',
np.sqrt(metrics.mean_squared_error(y_test,
pred_y)))
```

Multiple Linear Regression

You now know how to do Linear Regression when you have two variables. However, this is not a true reflection of what we have in the real world. Most of the problems the world is facing involve more than two variables. This explains why you need to learn Multiple Linear Regression.

The steps between the two are almost the same. However, the difference comes when it comes to evaluation. When evaluating the multiple linear regression model, we need to know the factor with the highest impact on the output variable. We also need to determine the relationship between the various variables.

We need to demonstrate this by prediction the consumption of fuel in US states. We will consider factors like per capita income, gas taxes, paved highways and the proportion of persons who have a driver's license.

Let us first import the libraries that we need to use:

```
import numpy as np
import pandas as pd
import matplotlib.pyplot as plt
```

I have saved the dataset with the name *fuel_consumption.csv* and kept it in the same directory where I have saved the Python script. Let us load the dataset:

dataset = pd.read_csv('fuel_consumption.csv')

Run the *head()* function to see what is contained in the dataset:

print(dataset.head())

Again, you may get an error for trying to print the contents of the dataset. Use the method we used previously to solve the problem. You should have the following code:

```
import numpy as np
import pandas as pd
import matplotlib.pyplot as plt
import sys
sys.__stdout__ = sys.stdout
dataset = pd.read_csv('fuel_consumption.csv')
print(dataset.head())
```

The code returns the following:

```
     Tax   Income  Highways  Licence  Consumption
0    9.0     3571      1976    0.525          541
1    9.0     4092      1250    0.572          524
2    9.0     3865      1586    0.580          561
3    7.5     4870      2351    0.529          414
4    8.0     4399       431    0.544          410
>>> |
```

Those are the first five rows of the dataset. Let us see the shape of the dataset:

print(dataset.shape)

```
>>> print(dataset.shape)
(48, 5)
>>>
```

Call the *describe()* function to see the statistical details of the dataset:

print(dataset.describe())

```
>>> print(dataset.describe())
             Tax        Income      Highways    Licence  Consumption
count  48.000000    48.000000     48.000000  48.000000    48.000000
mean    7.668333  4241.833333   5565.416667   0.570333   576.770833
std     0.950770   573.623768   3491.507166   0.055470   111.885816
min     5.000000  3063.000000    431.000000   0.451000   344.000000
25%     7.000000  3739.000000   3110.250000   0.529750   509.500000
50%     7.500000  4298.000000   4735.500000   0.564500   568.500000
75%     8.125000  4578.750000   7156.000000   0.595250   632.750000
max    10.000000  5342.000000  17782.000000   0.724000   968.000000
>>> |
```

Data Preparation

In the example of simple linear regression, we subdivided the data into attributes and labels. In this case, we will be directly using the column names for this purpose. Run the code given below:

```
X = dataset[['Tax', 'Income', 'Highways',
        'Licence']]
```

49

```
y = dataset['Consumption']
```

We have four columns for the attributes (the independent variables) and one column for the label (the dependent variable).

Let us now subdivide the data into training and test sets. 80% of the data will be used as the training set while the remaining 20% will be used as the test set:

First, let us import the *train_test_split()* method from Scikit-Learn:

from sklearn.model_selection import train_test_split

Run the following command to do the division of the data:

```
X_train, X_test, y_train, y_test =
train_test_split(X, y, test_size=0.2,
random_state=0)
```

We have the training and the test datasets.

Training the Algorithm

We now need to train the algorithm. This can be done by calling the *fit()* method as we did previously. Let us first import the *LinearRegression* class from the Scikit-Learn library:

from sklearn.linear_model import LinearRegression

Next, create an instance of the above class then use it to call the *fit()* method:

```
linear_regressor = LinearRegression()
linear_regressor.fit(X_train, y_train)
```

Note that this is a multiple linear regression and we are having many variables. The linear regression model has to find the optimal coefficients for each attribute. You can see the chosen coefficients by running the following command:

```
coeff = pd.DataFrame(linear_regressor.coef_,
X.columns, columns=['Coefficient'])
print(coeff)
```

The code returns the following:

```
            Coefficient
Tax          -40.016660
Income        -0.065413
Highways      -0.004741
Licence     1341.862121
```

This means that any unit increase in fuel Tax will lead to a decrease of 40.02 million gallons in the gas Consumption. Also, a unit increase in the proportion of the population with Driver's license will lead to an increase of 1.342 billion gallons in gas Consumption. The results also show that average Income and Highways have a very small impact on gas Consumption.

Predicting

We will make the predictions using the test data. The following script can help us do this:

```
pred_y = linear_regressor.predict(X_test)
```

At this point, you have the actual X_text values as well as the predicted values. We need to perform a comparison between these two to determine their similarities and differences. This can be done by running the following script:

```
df = pd.DataFrame({'Actual': y_test,
'Predicted': pred_y})
print(df)
```

The script returns the following output:

```
      Actual    Predicted
29       534    469.391989
4        410    545.645464
26       577    589.668394
30       571    569.730413
32       577    649.774809
37       704    646.631164
34       487    511.608148
40       587    672.475177
7        467    502.074782
10       580    501.270734
```

Evaluating the Accuracy of the Algorithm

We now need to evaluate the algorithm in terms of performance. This can be done by determining the values for the various types of errors. These include the MAE, RMSE, and MSE. This requires us to firm import the *metrics* class from Scikit-Learn as follows:

from sklearn import metrics

The calculation of the error values can then be done using the following script:

```
print('MAE:',
metrics.mean_absolute_error(y_test, pred_y))
print('MSE:', metrics.mean_squared_error(y_test,
pred_y))
print('RMSE:',
np.sqrt(metrics.mean_squared_error(y_test,
pred_y)))
```

The code returns the following:

```
MAE: 56.822247479
MSE: 4666.34478759
RMSE: 68.3106491522
```

52

The value for the root means the square error is 68.31 as shown above. This is slightly greater than 10% of mean value for gas consumption in all the states. It is true that our algorithm was not very much accurate, but we can still use it to make predictions.

The big error could be brought by a number of factors. Maybe there was a need for more data. We have used data for only one year. Having data collected over multiple years could have helped us improve the accuracy of the model. Also, we had assumed that our data has a linear relationship. This could not be the case, hence the big error. I recommend that you visualize the data to see whether this is true. Also, the features we have used could not be correlated.

Chapter 5- k-Nearest Neighbors Algorithm

The KNN algorithm is highly used for building more complex classifiers. It is a simple algorithm but it has outperformed many powerful classifiers. That is why it is used in numerous applications data compression, economic forecasting, and genetics.

KNN is a supervised learning algorithm, which means that we are given a labeled dataset made up of training observations (x, y) and our goal is to determine the relationship between x and y. This means that we should find a function that x to y such that when we are given an input value for x, we are able to predict the corresponding value for y.

The concept behind the KNN algorithm is very simple. It calculates the distance of the new data point to all the other training data points. The distance can be of various types including Manhattan, Euclidean etc. The K-nearest data points are chosen, in which K can be any integer. Finally, the data point is assigned to the class in which most of the K data points belong to.

We will use a dataset named Iris. We had explored it previously. We will be using this to demonstrate how to implement the KNN algorithm. This dataset is made up of four attributes namely *sepal-width, sepal-length, petal-width* and *petal-length*. Each type of the iris plant has certain attributes. Our goal is to predict the class to which a plant belongs to. The dataset has three classes *Iris-setosa, Iris-versicolor,* and *Iris-virginica.*

First, import all the libraries that are needed:

```
import numpy as np
import pandas as pd
import matplotlib.pyplot as plt
```

We now need to load the dataset into our working environment. Download it from the following URL:

https://archive.ics.uci.edu/ml/machine-learning-databases/iris/iris.data

We need to load the dataset from the above URL and store it in a Pandas data frame. This following script will help us achieve this:

```
# create a variable for the dataset url
iris_url =
"https://archive.ics.uci.edu/ml/machine-
learning-databases/iris/iris.data"
# Assign column names to the dataset
iris_names = ['Slength', 'Swidth', 'Plength',
'Pwidth', 'Class']
# Load the dataset from the url into a pandas
dataframe
dataset = pd.read_csv(iris_url,
names=iris_names)
We can have a view of the first few rows of the
dataset:
print(dataset.head())
```

	Slength	Swidth	Plength	Pwidth	Class
0	5.1	3.5	1.4	0.2	Iris-setosa
1	4.9	3.0	1.4	0.2	Iris-setosa
2	4.7	3.2	1.3	0.2	Iris-setosa
3	4.6	3.1	1.5	0.2	Iris-setosa
4	5.0	3.6	1.4	0.2	Iris-setosa

The S is for Sepal while P is for Petal. For example, *Slength* represents *Sepal length* while *Plength* represents *Petal length*.

If you get an error, remember to import the *sys* package and use it as shown below:

```
import numpy as np
import pandas as pd
```

```
import matplotlib.pyplot as plt
import sys
sys.__stdout__ = sys.stdout
url = "https://archive.ics.uci.edu/ml/machine-
learning-databases/iris/iris.data"
# Assign colum names to our dataset
names = ['Slength', 'Swidth', 'Plength',
'Pwidth', 'Class']
# Read the dataset to a pandas dataframe
dataset = pd.read_csv(url, names=names)
```

As usual, we should divide the dataset into attributes and labels. This can be done by running the following code:

```
X = dataset.iloc[:, :-1].values
y = dataset.iloc[:, 4].values
```

The variable X will hold the first four columns of the dataset which are the attributes while the variable y will hold the labels.

Splitting the Dataset

We need to be able to tell how well our algorithm performed. This will be done during the testing phase. This means that we should have training and testing data. We need to split the data into such two parts. 80% of the data will be used as the training set while 20% will be used as the test set.

Let us first import the *train_test_split* method from Scikit-Learn:

from sklearn.model_selection import train_test_split

We can then split the two as follows:

```
X_train, X_test, y_train, y_test =
train_test_split(X, y, test_size=0.20)
```

Feature Scaling

Before we can make the actual predictions, it is a good idea for us to scale the features. After that, all the features will be evaluated uniformly. Scikit-Learn comes with a class named *StandardScaler* which can help us perform the feature scaling. Let us first import this class:

from sklearn.preprocessing import StandardScaler

We then instantiate the class then use it to fit a model based on it:

```
feature_scaler = StandardScaler()
feature_scaler.fit(X_train)
X_train = feature_scaler.transform(X_train)
X_test = feature_scaler.transform(X_test)
```

The instance was given the name *feature_scaler*.

Training the Algorithm

With the Scikit-Learn library, it is easy for us to train the KNN algorithm. Let us first import the *KNeighborsClassifier* from the Scikit-Learn library:

from sklearn.neighbors import KNeighborsClassifier

The following code will help us train the algorithm:

```
knn_classifier =
KNeighborsClassifier(n_neighbors=5)
knn_classifier.fit(X_train, y_train)
```

Note that we have created an instance of the class we have created and named the instance *knn_classifier*. We have used one parameter in the instantiation, that is, *n_neighbors*. We have used 5 as the value of this parameter, and this basically denotes the value of K. Note that there is no specific value for K and it is chosen after testing and evaluation. However, for a start, 5 is used as the most popular value in most KNN applications.

We can then use the test data to make predictions. This can be done by running the script given below:

```
pred_y = knn_classifier.predict(X_test)
```

Evaluating the Accuracy of the Algorithm

Evaluation of the KNN algorithm is not done in the same way as evaluating the accuracy of the linear regression algorithm. We were using metrics like RMSE, MAE etc. In this case, we will use metrics like confusion matrix, precision, recall, and f1 score.

We can use the *classification_report* and *confusion_matrix* methods to calculate these metrics. Let us first import these from the Scikit-Learn library:

```
from sklearn.metrics import confusion_matrix,
classification_report
```

Run the following script:

```
print(confusion_matrix(y_test, pred_y))
print(classification_report(y_test, pred_y))
[[13  0  0]
 [ 0  5  0]
 [ 0  3  9]]
```

	precision	recall	f1-score	support
Iris-setosa	1.00	1.00	1.00	13
Iris-versicolor	0.62	1.00	0.77	5
Iris-virginica	1.00	0.75	0.86	12
avg / total	0.94	0.90	0.90	30

The results given above shows that the KNN algorithm did a good job in classifying the 30 records that we have in the test dataset. The results show that the average accuracy of the algorithm on the dataset was about 90%. This is not a bad percentage.

Comparing K Value with the Error Rate

We earlier said that there is no specific value of K that can be said that it gives the best results on the first go. We chose 5 because it is the most popular value used for K. The best way to find the best value of K is by plotting a graph of K value and the corresponding error for the dataset.

Let us create a plot using the mean error for predicted values of the test set for all the K values that range between 1 and 40. We should begin by calculating the mean of error for the predicted value with K ranging between 1 and 40. Just run the script given below:

```
error = []
# K values range between 1 and 40
for x in range(1, 40):
    knn = KNeighborsClassifier(n_neighbors=x)
    knn.fit(X_train, y_train)
    pred_x = knn.predict(X_test)
    error.append(np.mean(pred_x != y_test))
```

The code will run the loop from 1 to 40. In every iteration, the mean error for the predicted value of the test set is calculated and the result is appended to *error* list.

We should now plot the values of *error* against the values of K. The plot can be created by running the script given below:

```
plt.figure(figsize=(12, 6))
plt.plot(range(1, 40), error, color='blue',
linestyle='dashed', marker='o',
        markerfacecolor='blue', markersize=10)
```

```
plt.title('Error Rate for K')
plt.xlabel('K Values')
plt.ylabel('Mean Error')
plt.show()
```

The code generates the plot given below:

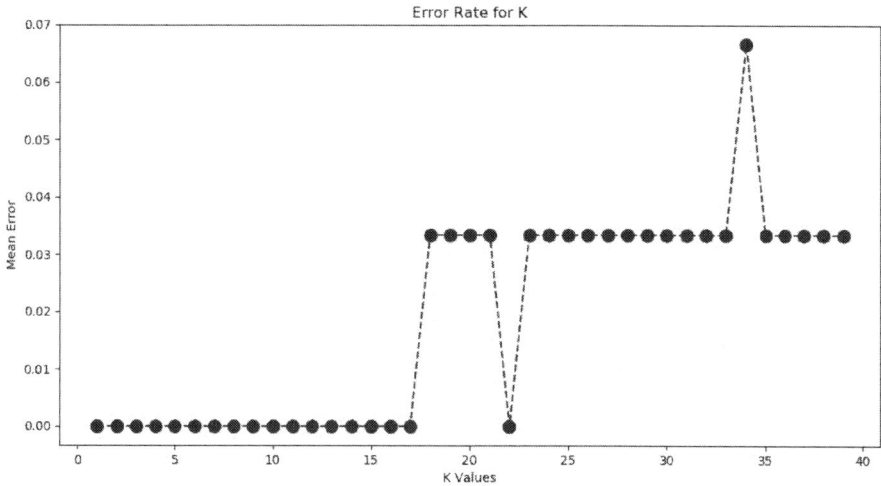

The graph shows that we will get a Mean Error of 0 when we use values of K between 1 and 17. It will then be good for you to play around with the value of K and see its impact on the accuracy of the predictions.

Chapter 6- K-Means Clustering

Clustering falls under the category of unsupervised machine learning algorithms. It is often applied when the data is not labeled. The goal of the algorithm is to identify clusters or groups within the data.

The idea behind the clusters is that the objects contained one cluster is more related to one another than the objects in the other clusters. The similarity is a metric reflecting the strength of the relationship between two data objects. Clustering is highly applied in exploratory data mining. In have many uses in diverse fields such as pattern recognition, machine learning, information retrieval, image analysis, data compression, bio-informatics, and computer graphics.

The algorithm forms clusters of data based on the similarity between data values. You are required to specify the value of K, which are the number of clusters that you expect the algorithm to make from the data. The algorithm first selects a centroid value for every cluster. After that, it performs three steps in an iterative manner:

1. Calculate the Euclidian distance between every data instance and the centroids for all clusters.
2. Assign the instances of data to the cluster of centroid with the nearest distance.
3. Calculate the new centroid values depending on the mean values of the coordinates of the data instances from the corresponding cluster.

Let us manually demonstrate how this algorithm works before implementing it on Scikit-Learn:

Suppose we have two dimensional data instances given below and by the name D:

```
D = { (5,3), (10,15), (15,12), (24,10), (30,45),
(85,70), (71,80), (60,78), (55,52), (80,91) }
```

Our goal is to divide the data into two clusters, namely C1 and C2 depending on the similarity between the data points.

We should first initialize the values for the centroids of both clusters, and this should be done randomly. The centroids will be named `c1` and `c2` for clusters `C1` and `C2` respectively, and we will initialize them with the values for the first two data points, that is, `(5,3)` and `(10,15)`. It is after this that you should begin the iterations.

Anytime that you calculate the Euclidean distance, the data point should be assigned to the cluster with the shortest Euclidean distance. Let us take the example of the data point `(5,3)` :

Euclidean Distance from the Cluster Centroid `c1 = (5,3) = 0`

Euclidean Distance from the Cluster Centroid `c2 = (10,15) = 13`

The Euclidean distance for the data point from point centroid `c1` is shorter compared to the distance of the same data point from centroid `c2`. This means that this data point will be assigned to the cluster `C1`.

Let us take another data point, `(15,12)` :

Euclidean Distance from the Cluster Centroid `c1 = (5,3)` is `13.45`

Euclidean Distance from the Cluster Centroid c2 = (10,15) is 5.83

The distance from the data point to the centroid c2 is shorter, hence it will be assigned to the cluster C2.

Now that the data points have been assigned to the right clusters, the next step should involve calculation of the new centroid values. The values should be calculated by determining the means of the coordinates for the data points belonging to a certain cluster.

If for example for C1 we had allocated the following two data points to the cluster:

(5, 3) and (24, 10). The new value for x coordinate will be the mean of the two:

```
x = (5 + 24) / 2
x = 14.5
The new value for y will be:
y = (3 + 10) / 2
y = 13/2
y = 6.5
```

The new centroid value for the c1 will be (14.5, 6.5).

This should be done for c2 and the entire process be repeated. The iterations should be repeated until when the centroid values do not update any more. This means if for example, you do three iterations, you may find that the updated values for centroids c1 and c2 in the fourth iterations are equal to what we had in iteration 3. This means that your data cannot be clustered any further.

You are now familiar with how the K-Means algorithm works. Let us discuss how you can implement it in the Scikit-Learn library.

Let us first import all the libraries that we need to use:

```
import matplotlib.pyplot as plt
import numpy as np
from sklearn.cluster import KMeans
```

Data Preparation

We should now prepare the data that is to be used. We will be creating a numpy array with a total of 10 rows and 2 columns. So, why have we chosen to work with a numpy array? It is because Scikit-Learn library can work with the numpy array data inputs without the need for preprocessing. Let us create it:

```
X = np.array([[5,3], [10,15], [15,12], [24,10],
[30,45], [85,70], [71,80], [60,78], [55,52],
[80,91],])
```

Visualizing the Data

Now that we have the data, we can create a plot and see how the data points are distributed. We will then be able to tell whether there are any clusters at the moment:

```
plt.scatter(X[:,0],X[:,1], label='True
Position')
plt.show()
```

The code gives the following plot:

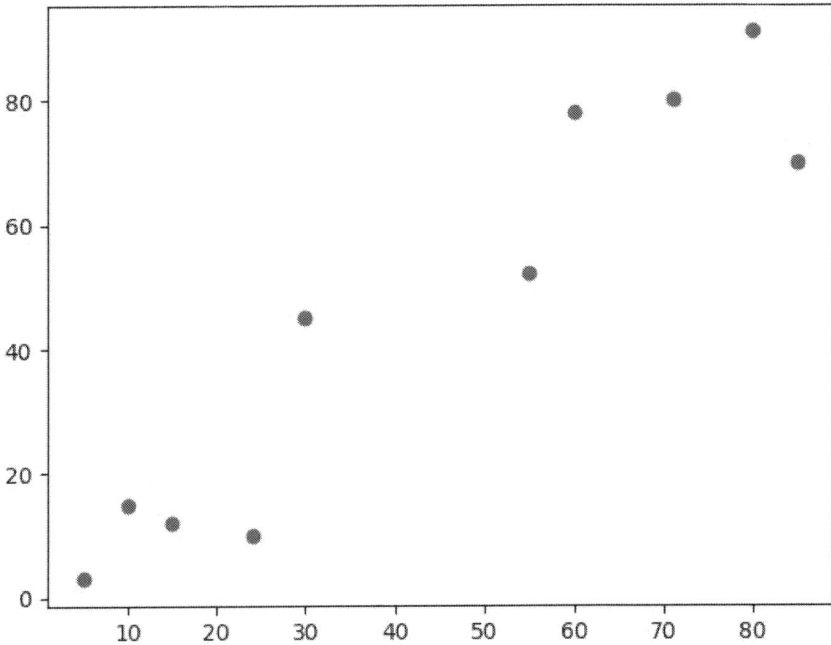

If we use our eyes, we will probably make two clusters from the above data, one at the bottom with five points and another one at the top with five points. We now need to investigate whether this is what the K-Means clustering algorithm will do.

Creating Clusters

We have seen that we can form two clusters from the data points, hence the value of K is now 2. These two clusters can be created by running the following code:

```
kmeans_clusters = KMeans(n_clusters=2)
kmeans_clusters.fit(X)
```

We have created an object named *kmeans_clusters* and 2 have been used as the value for the parameter *n_clusters*. We have then called the *fit()* method on this object and passed the data we have in our numpy array as the parameter to the method.

We can now have a look at the centroid values that the algorithm has created for the final clusters:

```
print (kmeans_clusters.cluster_centers_)
```
This returns the following:

```
[[ 16.8   17. ]
 [ 70.2   74.2]]
```

The first row above gives us the coordinates for the first centroid, which is, (16.8, 17). The second row gives us the coordinates of the second centroid, which is, (70.2, 74.2). If you followed the manual process of calculating the values of these, they should be the same. This will be an indication that the K-Means algorithm worked well.

The following script will help us see the data point labels:

```
print(kmeans_clusters.labels_)
```
This returns the following:

```
[0 0 0 0 0 1 1 1 1 1]
```

The above output shows a one-dimensional array of 10 elements which correspond to the clusters that are assigned to the 10 data points. You clearly see that we first have a sequence of zeroes which shows that the first 5 points have been clusterd together while the last five points have been clustered together. Note that the 0 and 1 have no mathematical significance but they have simply been used to represent the cluster IDs. If we had three clusters, then the last one would have been represented using 2's.

We can now plot the data points and see how they have been clustered. We need to plot the data points alongside their assigned labels to be able to distinguish the clusters. Just execute the script given below:

```
plt.scatter(X[:,0],X[:,1],
c=kmeans_clusters.labels_, cmap='rainbow')
plt.show()
```

The script returns the following plot:

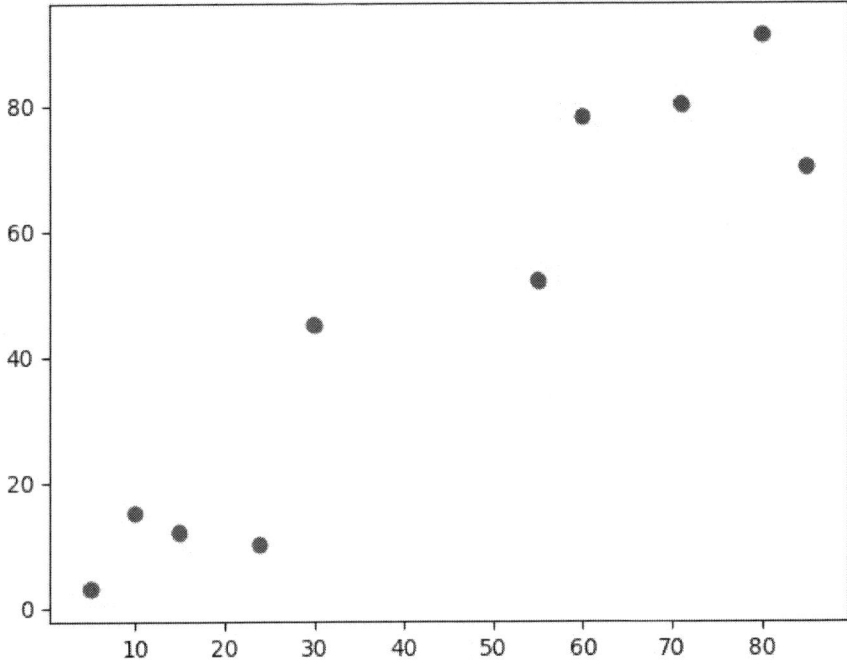

We have simply plotted the first column of the array named X against the second column. At the same time, we have passed *kmeans_labels_* as the value for parameter c which corresponds to the labels. Note the use of the parameter *cmap='rainbow'*. This parameter helps us to choose the color type for the different data points.

As you expected, the first five points have been clustered together at the bottom left and assigned a similar color. The remaining five points have been clustered together at the top right and assigned one unique color.

We can choose to plot the points together with the centroid coordinates for every cluster to see how the positioning of the centroid affects clustering. Let us use three clusters to see how they affect the centroids. The following script will help you to create the plot:

```
plt.scatter(X[:,0], X[:,1],
c=kmeans_clusters.labels_, cmap='rainbow')
plt.scatter(kmeans_clusters.cluster_centers_[:,0
] ,kmeans_clusters.cluster_centers_[:,1],
color='black')
plt.show()
```

The script returns the following plot:

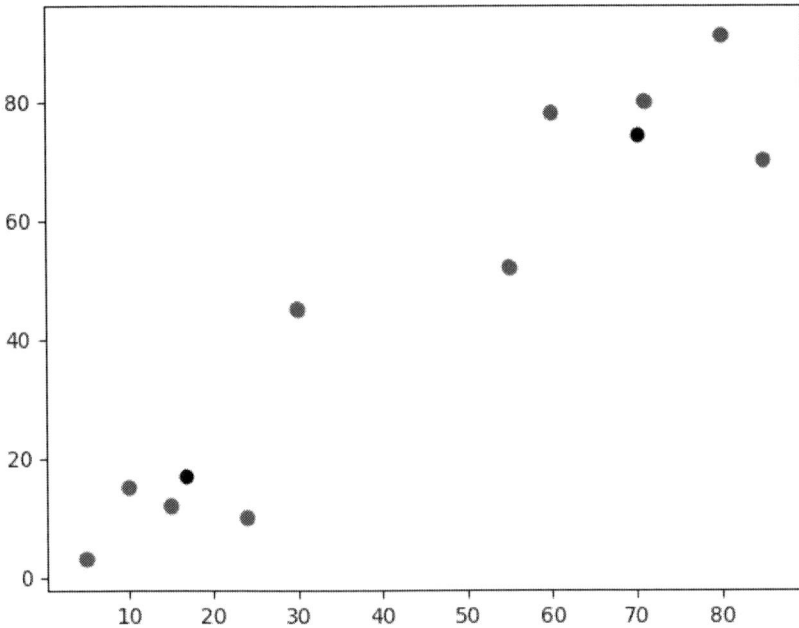

We have chosen to plot the centroid points in black color.

Chapter 7- Support Vector Machines

SVMs fall under the category of supervised machine learning algorithms and are highly applied classification and regression problems. It is known for its ability to handle nonlinear input spaces. It is highly applied in applications like intrusion detection, face detection, classification of news articles, emails and web pages, handwriting recognition and classification of genes.

The algorithm works by segregating the data points in the best way possible. The distance between the nearest points is referred to as the *margin*. The goal is to choose a hyperplane with the maximum possible margin between the support vectors in a given dataset.

To best understand how this algorithm works, let us first implement it in Scikit-Learn library. Our goal is to predict whether a bank currency note is fake or authentic. We will use the attributes of the note including variance of the image, the skewness of the wavelet transformed image, curtosis of the image and entropy of the image. Since this is a binary classification algorithm, let us use the SVM classification algorithm.

If we have a linearly separable data with two dimensions, the goal of a typical machine learning algorithm is to identify a boundary that will divide the data so as to minimize the misclassification error. In most cases, one gets several lines with all these lines correctly classifying the data.

SVM is different from the other classification algorithms in the way it selects the decision boundary maximizing the distance from the nearest data points for all classes. The goal of SVM is not to find the decision boundary only, but to find the most optimal decision boundary.

The most optimal decision boundary refers to the decision boundary with the maximum margin from nearest points of all classes. The nearest points from the decision boundary maximizing the distance between the decision boundary and the points are known as *support vectors*. For the case of support vector machines, the decision boundary is known as *maximum margin classifier* or *maximum margin hyper plane*.

A complex mathematics is involved in the calculation of the support vectors; determine the margin between the decision boundary and support vectors and maximizing the margin.

Let us begin by importing the necessary libraries:

```
import numpy as np
import pandas as pd
import matplotlib.pyplot as plt
```

This dataset can be downloaded from the following URL:

https://drive.google.com/file/d/13nw-uRXPY8XIZQxKRNZ3yYlho-CYm_Qt/view

Download and store it on your local machine. I have saved the file in the same directory as my Python scripts and given it the name *bank_note.csv*.

Importing the Dataset

We will use the *read_csv* method provided by the Pandas library to read the data and import it into our workspace. This can be done as follows:

```
dataset = pd.read_csv("bank_note.csv")
```

Let us call the *shape* method to print the shape of the data for us:

```
print(dataset.shape)
```
This returns the following:

```
(1372, 5)
```

This shows that there are 1372 columns and 5 columns in the dataset. Let us print the first 5 rows of the dataset:

```
print(dataset.head())
```

Again, this may return an error because of lack of the output information. Let us solve this using the Python's sys library. You should now have the following code:

```
import numpy as np
import pandas as pd
import matplotlib.pyplot as plt
import sys
sys.__stdout__=sys.stdout
dataset = pd.read_csv("bank_note.csv")
print(dataset.head())
```

The code returns the following output:

```
   Variance  Skewness  Curtosis  Entropy  Class
0   3.62160    8.6661   -2.8073 -0.44699      0
1   4.54590    8.1674   -2.4586 -1.46210      0
2   3.86600   -2.6383    1.9242  0.10645      0
3   3.45660    9.5228   -4.0112 -3.59440      0
4   0.32924   -4.4552    4.5718 -0.98880      0
```

All attributes of the data are numeric as shown above. Even the last attribute is numeric as its values are either 0 or 1.

Preprocessing the Data

It is now time to subdivide the above data into attributes and labels as well as training and test sets. The following code will help us subdivide the data into attributes and labels:

```
X = dataset.drop('Class', axis=1)
y = dataset['Class']
```

The first line above helps us store all the columns of the dataset into variable X, except the *class* column. The *drop()* function has helped us exclude the *Class* column from this. The second line has then helped us store the *Class* column into variable *y*. The variable X now has attributes while the variable *y* now has the corresponding labels.

We have achieved the goal of diving the dataset into attributes and labels. The next step is to divide the dataset into training and test sets. Scikit-learn has a library known as *model_selection* which provides us with a method named *train_test_split* that we can use to divide the data into training and test sets.

First, let us import the *train_test_split* method:

```
from sklearn.model_selection import
train_test_split
```

The following script will then help us to perform the split:

```
X_train, X_test, y_train, y_test =
train_test_split(X, y, test_size = 0.20)
```

Training the Algorithm

Now that the data has been split into training and test sets, we should now train the SVM on the training set. Scikit-Learn comes with a library known as *svm* which has built-in classes for various SVM algorithms.

In this case, we will be doing a classification task, hence we will use the support vector classifier class (SVC). The takes a single parameter, that is, the kernel type. For a simple SVM, the parameter should be set to "linear" since the simple SVMs can only classify data that is linearly separable.

We will call the *fit* method of SVC to train the algorithm on our training set. The training set should be passed as a parameter to the *fit* method. Let us first import the SVC class from Scikit-Learn:

```
from sklearn.svm import SVC
```

Now run the following code:

```
svc_classifier = SVC(kernel='linear')
svc_classifier.fit(X_train, y_train)
```

Making Predicting

We should use the SVC class for making predictions. Note that the predictions will be made on the test data. Here is the code for making predictions:

```
pred_y = svc_classifier.predict(X_test)
```

Evaluating the Accuracy of the Algorithm

In classification tasks, we use confusion matrix, recall, precision and F1 as the metrics. Scikit-Learn has the *metrics* library which provides us with the *confusion_matrix* and *classification_report* methods which can help us find the values of these metrics. The following code can help us find the value for these metrics:

First, let us import the above methods from the Scikit-Learn library:

```
from sklearn.metrics import confusion_matrix,
classification_report
```

Here is the code that can help in doing the evaluation:

```
print(confusion_matrix(y_test,pred_y))
print(classification_report(y_test,pred_y))
```

The code returns the following:

```
[[160    1]
 [  1 113]]
                precision    recall  f1-score   support

            0       0.99      0.99      0.99       161
            1       0.99      0.99      0.99       114

avg / total       0.99      0.99      0.99       275
```

The output given above shows that the algorithm did a good task. An average of 99% for the above metrics is not bad.

Let us give another example of how to implement SVM in Scikit-Learn using the Iris dataset. We had already loaded the Iris dataset, a dataset that shows details of flowers in terms of sepal and petal measurements, that is, width and length. We can now learn from the data, and then make a prediction for unknown data. These calls for us to create an estimator then call its fit method.

This is demonstrated in the script given below:

```
from sklearn import svm
from sklearn import datasets
# Loading the dataset
iris = datasets.load_iris()
clf = svm.LinearSVC()
# learn from the dataset
clf.fit(iris.data, iris.target)
# predict unseen data
```

```
clf.predict([[ 6.2,   4.2,   3.5,   0.35]])
# Changing model parameters using the attributes
ending with an underscore
print(clf.coef_ )
```

The code will return the following output:

```
[[ 0.18423824   0.45123312  -0.80793878  -0.45071592]
 [ 0.05187834  -0.88969839   0.40345845  -0.93664852]
 [-0.85062306  -0.98667154   1.38105171   1.86536558]]
```

We now have the predicted values for our data. Note that we imported both *datasets* and *svm* from the scikit-learn library. After loading the dataset, a model was fitted/created by learning patterns from the data. This was done by calling the *fit()* method. Note that the *LinearSVC()* method helps us to create an estimator for the support vector classifier, on which we are to create the model. We have then passed in new data for which we need to make a prediction.

Chapter 8- Neural Networks with Scikit-learn

Neural networks are a machine learning framework that tries to mimic the way the natural biological neural networks operate. Humans have the capacity of identifying patterns with a very high degree of accuracy. Anytime you see a cow, you can immediately recognize that it is a cow. This also applies to when you see a goat. The reason is that you have learned over a period of time how a cow or a goat looks like and what differentiates between the two.

Artificial neural networks refer to computation systems that try to imitate the capabilities of human learning via a complex architecture that resembles the nervous system of a human being.

The structure of Neuron

A neutron is made up of the cell body, having a number of extensions from it. Majority of these are in the form of branches commonly known as "dendrites".

A long process or a branching exists, and this is referred to as the "axon". The transmission of signals begins at a region in this axon, and this region is known as the "hillock".

The neuron has a boundary which is known as the "cell membrane". A potential difference exists between the inside and the outside of the cell membrane. This is known as the "membrane potential".

If the input becomes large enough, some action potential will be generated. This action potential then travels will then travel down the axon and away from the cell body.

A neuron is connected to another neuron by synapses. The information leaves the neuron via an axon and is then passed to the synapses and to the neuron which is expected to receive it. Note that a neuron will only fire once the threshold exceeds a certain amount. The signals are very important as they are received by the other neurons. The neurons use the signals or the spikes for communication. The spikes are also responsible for encoding the information which is being sent.

Synapses can either be inhibitory or excitatory. When spikes arrive at the excitatory synapse, the receiving neuron will be caused to fire. If the signals are received at an inhibitory synapse, then the receiving neuron is inhibited from firing.

The synapses and the cell body usually calculate the difference the incoming inhibitory and excitatory inputs. If this difference is found to be too large, the neuron will be made to fire.

Back Propagation

For you to train a neural network to perform a task, the units of each unit must be adjusted so that we can reduce the error between the actual output and the target output. This means that the derivative of the weights must be computed by the network. To make it simple, the network has to monitor the changes in error as the weights are being increased or decreased. The *backpropagation* algorithm is the one which is widely used in the calculation of this error.

If you are having your network units being linear, then this algorithm will be easy for you to understand. For the algorithm to get the error derivative of the weights, it should first determine the rate at which the error is changing as the unit's activity level is being changed. For the case of the output units, the error derivative is obtained by determining the different between the real and the target output. To find the error change rate for the hidden unit in a layer which id before the output layer, all weights between the hidden unit and the output units which it has been connected to have to be determined. We can then go ahead and multiple the weights by error derivatives in the weights and then the product is added together. The sum you get will be equal to the error change rate for the hidden unit. Once you have obtained the error change rate in the weights of the hidden layer which is just before the output layer, we will be capable of calculating the error change rate for the other layers. The calculation of this for these will be done from layer to the next layer, and in a direction which is opposite to the direction in which the activities are usually transmitted through the network. This explains where the name back propagation" comes from. After the error change rate has been calculated for some unit, the error derivative for the weights for all the incoming connections of the weight can be calculated more easily. The error derivative for the weights can be obtained by multiplying the rate of error change with the activity via the incoming connection.

Implementation

We need to implement a neural network with Scikit-Learn in Python. We will use the *iris* dataset for this task. We will be getting this dataset from the following link:

https://archive.ics.uci.edu/ml/machine-learning-databases/iris/iris.data

First, import the necessary libraries into your workspace:

```
import numpy as np
import pandas as pd
import matplotlib.pyplot as plt
Next, let us load the data from the above URL
into the pandas data frame:
# create a variable for the dataset url
```

```
iris_url =
"https://archive.ics.uci.edu/ml/machine-
learning-databases/iris/iris.data"
# Assign column names to the dataset
names = ['Slength', 'Swidth', 'Plength',
'Pwidth', 'Class']
# Load the dataset from the url into a pandas
dataframe
dataset = pd.read_csv(iris_url,
names=iris_names)
```

Note that the dataset has been loaded into a pandas data frame named dataset and columns have also been assigned to the dataset. Let us call the head() function on the data to be sure it has been loaded:

```
print(dataset.head())
```

You may get an error. Solve it by writing the code as follows:

```
import numpy as np
import pandas as pd
import matplotlib.pyplot as plt
import sys
sys.__stdout__ = sys.stdout
# create a variable for the dataset url
iris_url =
"https://archive.ics.uci.edu/ml/machine-
learning-databases/iris/iris.data"
# Assign column names to the dataset
iris_names = ['Slength', 'Swidth', 'Plength',
'Pwidth', 'Class']
# Load the dataset from the url into a pandas
dataframe
dataset = pd.read_csv(iris_url,
names=iris_names)
print(dataset.head())
```

The code will return the following:

	Slength	Swidth	Plength	Pwidth	Class
0	5.1	3.5	1.4	0.2	Iris-setosa
1	4.9	3.0	1.4	0.2	Iris-setosa
2	4.7	3.2	1.3	0.2	Iris-setosa
3	4.6	3.1	1.5	0.2	Iris-setosa
4	5.0	3.6	1.4	0.2	Iris-setosa

This shows that the data was loaded successfully.

Preprocessing the Data

The dataset has 5 columns, and our goal is to predict the fifth column, that is, Class. Let us subdivide the dataset into attributes and labels:

```
X = dataset.iloc[:, 0:4]
y = dataset.select_dtypes(include=[object])
```

The data in the first four columns have been assigned to the variable X. These are the attributes. The data in the fifth column has been assigned to variable y. This forms the label.

You can have a look of how variable y looks like by running the following command:

y.head()

```
>>> y.head()
         Class
0   Iris-setosa
1   Iris-setosa
2   Iris-setosa
3   Iris-setosa
4   Iris-setosa
>>>
```

You can see that the variable y has categorical values. However, the neural networks are known to work well with numerical data, hence we should convert the above into numerical values. First, let us see the number of unique values that we have in variable y:

```
y.Class.unique()
```

```
>>> y.Class.unique()

array(['Iris-setosa', 'Iris-versicolor', 'Iris-virginica'], dtype=object)
>>>
```

The above output shows that we have three unique categories, that is, the Iris-setosa, Iris-versicolor, and Iris-virginia. We should convert these into numerical values. This can be done using the Scikit-Learn's class named *LabelEncoder.*

Let us first import the *preprocessing* method from Scikit-Learn:

```
from sklearn import preprocessing
```

The following code can then help us do the conversion:

```
lab = preprocessing.LabelEncoder()
y = y.apply(lab.fit_transform)
```

We can now check for the unique values of the variable y:

```
y.Class.unique()
```

```
>>> y.Class.unique()
array([0, 1, 2], dtype=int64)
>>> |
```

It is now clear that the categorical values have been converted into numerical values, that is, 0, 1 and 2.

We should now split the data into the training and test sets. This will help us prevent the problem of *overfitting.* The training set will be used to train the data while the test data will be used to evaluate the performance of the neural network model.

Let us first import the *train_test_split* method from Scikit-Learn:

```
from sklearn.model_selection import
train_test_split
```

The following script will then help us perform the split:

```
X_train, X_test, y_train, y_test =
train_test_split(X, y, test_size = 0.20)
```

80% of the data will be used for training while 20% of the data will be used for testing.

Feature Scaling

Before we can make the actual predictions, it is recommended that we first scale the features so that they can be evaluated uniformly. Note that feature scaling should only be done on the training data but not on the test data. The reason is that real world data is not scaled and a neural network is geared towards making predictions on such data. That is why the test data should be kept as real as possible.

Let us first import the *StandardScaler* class from Scikit-Learn:

```
from sklearn.preprocessing import StandardScaler
```

Let us create an instance of the above class then call the *fit()* method on this instance:

```
feature_scaler = StandardScaler()
feature_scaler.fit(X_train)
X_train = feature_scaler.transform(X_train)
X_test = feature_scaler.transform(X_test)
```

Training the Algorithm and Making Predictions

We now need to train the neural network that will be able to be used for making predictions. We should first import the *MLPClassifier* from the neural network library of Scikit-Learn. This can be done as follows:

```
from sklearn.neural_network import MLPClassifier
```

The following code can then help us do the training of the neural network:

```
mlp_classifier =
MLPClassifier(hidden_layer_sizes=(10, 10, 10),
max_iter=1000)
mlp_classifier.fit(X_train,
y_train.values.ravel())
```

We have just used three lines of code to create a neural network. That is great! Notice the use of the *hidden_layer_sizes* parameter. We have used it to create three hidden layers for the network each with 10 nodes. There is no rule that limits from choosing only a certain number of layers and nodes for your neural network. These vary depending on the nature of the problem in question. You can try a number of different combinations and see what works best for you.

We have also used the *max_iter* parameter. The purpose of this parameter is to set the number of iterations or epochs that you need your network to run. The "relu" activation function is used by default together with the "adam" cost optimizer. However, these functions can be changed using *activation* and *solver* parameters respectively.

We have then called the *fit* method which trains the algorithm on our training data, that is, X_train and y_train.

Now that algorithm has been trained on the training data, we can make predictions on the test data. This can be done by running the script given below:

```
predictions = mlp_classifier.predict(X_test)
```

Evaluation of the Accuracy of the Algorithm

The algorithm has been trained and predictions made on the test data. It is time for us to evaluate how well it performs. The evaluation will be done using metrics like confusion matrix, precision, recall, and f1 score. We should compare the values we got from the predictions to the actual values that were collected.

Let us first import the *classification_report* and *classification_matrix* methods of the Scikit-Learn's *metric* library:

```
from sklearn.metrics import confusion_matrix,
classification_report
```

The evaluation can then be done by running the following script:

```
print(confusion_matrix(y_test,predictions))
print(classification_report(y_test,predictions))
```

The script returns the following result:

```
[[ 8  0  0]
 [ 0 14  0]
 [ 0  1  7]]
```

	precision	recall	f1-score	support
0	1.00	1.00	1.00	8
1	0.93	1.00	0.97	14
2	1.00	0.88	0.93	8
avg / total	0.97	0.97	0.97	30

The above results are good. The confusion matrix shows that only one plant was misclassified out of all the 30 plants. We also have an f1-score of 0.97 which is good considering that we only had 150 instances to train the neural network on. Anytime you get an accuracy which 90% and above, you can conclude that the performance was good.

Chapter 9- Random Forest Algorithm

This is a type of supervised machine learning algorithm that works based on ensemble learning. Ensemble learning refers to the kind of learning in which different types of algorithms or one algorithm is joined multiple times to get a more powerful prediction model. The random forest algorithm is a combination of many algorithms of a similar type, that is, multiple decision trees, resulting into a forest of trees, explaining the source of the name "random forest". The random forest algorithm can be applied in both regression and classification problems.

How it Works

The random forest algorithm follows the following basic steps in its work:

1. Select N random records from a data set.
2. Build a decision tree from these N random records.
3. Select the number of trees that you need in the algorithm and repeat the above two steps.
4. If it is a regression problem, for a new record, every tree in the forest will predict a value for Y (the output). We can calculate the final value by taking the average of all predicted values by all trees in the forest. Or, for the case of a classification problem, every tree in the forest should predict the category under which the new record belongs. The new record is finally assigned to the category that has won the majority vote.

Random Forest and Regression Problems

In this chapter, we will be showing you how to solve regression problems using random forests in Scikit-Learn. We will be using the fuel consumption dataset we used previously. The gas consumption will be predicted based on factors like fuel tax (in cents), per capita income (in dollars), paved highways (miles) and percentage of the population with driver's license.

Let us first import the numpy and pandas libraries:

```
import pandas as pd
import numpy as np
```

I already have the dataset saved in the same directory as my Python script with the name *fuel_consumption.csv*. Run the following command to import into a Pandas data frame:

```
dataset = pd.read_csv('fuel_consumption.csv')
```

See what is contained in the dataset by running the *head()* function on the data:

```
print(dataset.head())
```

This may give you an error. Sort out the error as usual so that you end up with the following code:

```
import pandas as pd
import numpy as np
import sys
sys.__stdout__ =sys.stdout
dataset = pd.read_csv('fuel_consumption.csv')
print(dataset.head())
```

This returns the following:

	Tax	Income	Highways	Licence	Consumption
0	9.0	3571	1976	0.525	541
1	9.0	4092	1250	0.572	524
2	9.0	3865	1586	0.580	561
3	7.5	4870	2351	0.529	414
4	8.0	4399	431	0.544	410

The above data shows that the values are not scaled well. We will have to do this later.

Data Preparation

It is now time for us to split the dataset into what we need. First, we will split it into attributes and labels then into training and test sets. Here is the code for subdividing the data into attributes and labels:

```
X = dataset.iloc[:, 0:4].values
y = dataset.iloc[:, 4].values
```

We now need to divide the data into training and test sets. 80% of the data will be used for training while 20% will be used for testing the algorithm.

Let us first import the *train_test_split* method:

```
from sklearn.model_selection import
train_test_split
```

The following code will then do the splitting work:

```
X_train, X_test, y_train, y_test =
train_test_split(X, y, test_size=0.2,
random_state=0)
```

Feature Scaling

At this point, the dataset is not scaled well. The Income field, for example, has values ranging up to thousands while the Tax field has values ranging in tens. This is why we should scale our data. We will use the *StandardScaler* class provided by Scikit-Learn to scale the dataset. Let us first import this class:

```
from sklearn.preprocessing import StandardScaler
```

We can now create an instance of this class and use it for scaling the dataset:

```
rf_scaler = StandardScaler()
X_train = rf_scaler.fit_transform(X_train)
X_test = rf_scaler.transform(X_test)
```

The dataset is now scaled.

Training the Algorithm

We should now train the random forests algorithms to help us solve the regression problem. Let us first inform the *RandomForestRegressor* class:

```
from sklearn.ensemble import
RandomForestRegressor
```

We can now create an instance of the above class then use it to train the algorithm and make a prediction on the test dataset:

```
rf_regressor =
RandomForestRegressor(n_estimators=20,
random_state=0)
rf_regressor.fit(X_train, y_train)
pred_y = rf_regressor.predict(X_test)
```

Anytime that you need to solve a regression problem using the random forests algorithm, use the *RandomForestRegressor* class. Notice the use of the *n_estimators* parameter in the above example. It simply specifies the number of trees to be used in the random forest. We have started with a total of 20 trees to test ho our algorithm will work.

Evaluating Algorithm Performance

It is now time for us to evaluate how well the algorithm has performed on the dataset. This is a regression problem, so the metrics used to evaluate the performance of the algorithm include mean absolute error (MAE), mean squared error MSE), and root mean squared error (RMSE).

First, import the *metrics* method from the Scikit-Learn library:

```
from sklearn import metrics
```

The following script will then help you get the values of the above metrics:

```
print('MAE:',
metrics.mean_absolute_error(y_test, pred_y))
print('MSE:', metrics.mean_squared_error(y_test,
pred_y))
print('RMSE:',
np.sqrt(metrics.mean_squared_error(y_test,
pred_y)))
```

The code returns the following output:

```
MAE: 51.765
MSE: 4216.16675
RMSE: 64.932016371
```

We used 20 trees which have given us a root mean square value of 64.93. This value is greater than the 10 percent of the average fuel consumption. This is an indication that we did not use enough trees/estimators.

What you should know is that the values of the errors will decrease with an increase in the number of trees or estimators. This is why I recommend that you play around with this to see whether you can get good values for the errors. There are also other parameters that you can play around with.

Random Forest and Classification problems

We need to demonstrate how random forest can be used for solving classification problems. We will use the dataset for *bank_note* to predict whether a bank note is authentic or not. We will depend on four attributes of the note including variance of the image wavelet transformed image, entropy, skewness, and curtosis of the image.

Although this is a binary classification problem, we will be using a random forest classifier to solve it. Let us first import the libraries that we will need to solve the problem:

```
import numpy as np
import pandas as pd
```

I have saved the dataset with the name *bank_note.csv* and kept it in the same directory as my Python script. The following script can help me to import the dataset:

```
dataset = pd.read_csv("bank_note.csv")
```

Let us see the first 5 rows of the dataset:

```
print(dataset.head())
```

If you get an error, write the code as follows:

```
import numpy as np
import pandas as pd
import sys
sys.__stdout__ =sys.stdout
dataset = pd.read_csv("bank_note.csv")
print(dataset.head())
```

The code returns the following:

	Variance	Skewness	Curtosis	Entropy	Class
0	3.62160	8.6661	-2.8073	-0.44699	0
1	4.54590	8.1674	-2.4586	-1.46210	0
2	3.86600	-2.6383	1.9242	0.10645	0
3	3.45660	9.5228	-4.0112	-3.59440	0
4	0.32924	-4.4552	4.5718	-0.98880	0

In the regression problem, the dataset was not scaled well, and this is also the case with this classification problem. We will have to scale this data before we can train the algorithm.

Data Preparation

Run the following cod to split the data into attributes and labels:

```
X = dataset.iloc[:, 0:4].values
y = dataset.iloc[:, 4].values
```

We now need to split the data into training and test sets. Let us first import the *train_test_split* method from Scikit-Learn:

from sklearn.model_selection import train_test_split

Now run the following code to do the splitting:

```
X_train, X_test, y_train, y_test =
train_test_split(X, y, test_size=0.2,
random_state=0)
```

Feature Scaling

We will implement feature scaling in the same way we did for the regression problem. We will first import the *StandardScaler* class by running the following import statement:

```
from sklearn.preprocessing import StandardScaler
```

Then we run the following command:

```
sc = StandardScaler()
X_train = sc.fit_transform(X_train)
X_test = sc.transform(X_test)
```

Note that we first created an instance of the *StandardScaler* class then we have used it to perform the scaling on the data.

Training the Algorithm

Now that the data is scaled, the random forest algorithm can be trained to solve the classification problem. Remember that for the regression problem, we used the *RandomForestRegressor* class. For this calcification problem, we will use the *RandomForestClassifier* class. Let us begin by importing this class:

```
from sklearn.ensemble import
RandomForestClassifier
```

Here is the code for training the algorithm:

```
classifier =
RandomForestClassifier(n_estimators=20,
random_state=0)
classifier.fit(X_train, y_train)
pred_y = classifier.predict(X_test)
```

Note that we have also called the *n_estimators* parameter. Again, we have used 20 trees to train the algorithm.

Evaluating the Performance of the Algorithm

To evaluate the performance of a random forest classifier, we use metrics like accuracy, precision recall, confusion matrix, and F1 values. First, run the following import statement:

```
from sklearn.metrics import confusion_matrix,
classification_report, accuracy_score
```

You can then run the following command:

```
print(confusion_matrix(y_test,pred_y))
print(classification_report(y_test, pred_y))
print(accuracy_score(y_test, pred_y))
```

The code returns the following:

```
[[155    2]
 [  1  117]]
              precision    recall  f1-score   support

           0       0.99      0.99      0.99       157
           1       0.98      0.99      0.99       118

avg / total       0.99      0.99      0.99       275

0.989090909091
```

The above results show that the random forest classifier achieved an accuracy score of 98.91% when using 20 trees. 98.91% is a good score, so there is no need for us to increase the number of trees/estimators. If you need to improve the accuracy of this classifier, try to vary the other parameters other than the number of trees/estimators.

Chapter 10- Using TensorFlow

TensorFlow is a library for dataflow programming. It makes it easy for us to work with mathematical expressions. Now that you have installed TensorFlow, we need to use it.

To see whether TensorFlow has been installed on your system, try to import it by running the following command:

import tensorflow as tf

If it is not installed, you will get an error, otherwise, the installation as successful. If not installed, follow the steps we discussed earlier to install the library.

DataFlow Graphs

In TensorFlow, computation is based on graphs. The graphs provide us with an alternative to soling mathematical problems. Consider the expression given below:

```
x = ( y+z ) * ( z+4 )
```

The above expression may also be expressed as follows:

```
p=y + z
q= z + 4
x= p * q
```

When represented as above, it becomes easy to express the expression in the form of a graph. Initially, we had a single expression but we now have two expressions. The two expressions can be performed in parallel. We can gain from this in terms of computation time. Such gains are very important in deep learning and big data applications, especially in Convolutional Neural Networks (CNNs) and Recurrent Neural Networks (RNNs) which are all complicated neural network architectures.

The goal of TensorFlow is to implement graphs and help in the computation of operations in parallel which will lead to efficiency gains. In TensorFlow, the graph nodes are known as *tensors* and they are simply multi-dimensional data arrays. The graph begins with the input layer where we find the input tensor. After the input layer, we get the hidden layer which has rectified linear units as the activation function.

Constants

In TensorFlow, we create constants using the function constantly. This function constant has a signature *constant(value, dtype=None, shape=None, name='Const', verify_shape=False)*, in which *value* is the actual constant value to be used for further computation, *dtype* is a data type parameter such as int8/16, float32/64, *shape* denotes optional dimensions, *name* is optional name for the tensor while the last parameter is a Boolean indicating the verification of the shape of the values.

If you need constants with specific values in the training model, use the *constant object* as shown in the example given below:

```
k = tf.constant(5.2, name="x", dtype=tf.float32)
```

Variables

In TensorFlow, variables refer to in-memory buffers with tensors that should be initialized explicitly and used in-graph to maintain state across the session. When the constructor is called, the variable is added to the computational graph.

Variables are mostly used when starting with training models, and they are used for holding and updating parameters. The initial values that is passed as the argument to the constructor represents the tensor or object that is to be converted or returned as a tensor. This means that if we need to fill a variable with some predefined or random values that are to be used later in the training process and updated over the iterations, it can be defined in the following way:

```
m = tf.Variable(tf.zeros([1]), name="m")
```

In TensorFlow, variables can also be used in calculations whereby the variable is not trainable and it is definable as follows:

```
m = tf.Variable(tf.add(x, y), trainable=False)
```

Sessions

For us to evaluate the nodes, the computational graph must be run within a session. The purpose of a session is to encapsulate the state and control of a TensorFlow runtime. If the session doesn't have parameters, it will use the default graph that was created in the current session; otherwise, the session class will accept the graph parameter, which is used in the session to be executed.

Let us run the *hello* code in TensorFlow:

```
import tensorflow as tf
h = tf.constant('Hello, this is TensorFlow!')
s = tf.Session()
print(s.run(h))
```

The code returns the following:

```
Hello, this is TensorFlow!
```

In the example given below, we are using all the terms defined above to calculate a very simple linear function in TensorFlow:

import tensorflow as tf

```
y = tf.constant(-2.0, name="y",
dtype=tf.float32)
a = tf.constant(5.0, name="a", dtype=tf.float32)
b = tf.constant(13.0, name="b",
dtype=tf.float32)
z = tf.Variable(tf.add(tf.multiply(a, y), b))
init = tf.global_variables_initializer()
with tf.Session() as session:
    session.run(init)
    print session.run(z)
```

The code returns the following:

```
3.0
```

Placeholders

Suppose we are not aware of the value of array *y* during declaration phase of our TensorFlow problem, that is, before the stage for *tf.Session()* as *ses*. In such a case, TensorFlow expects us to declare basic structure of our data by use of *tf.placeholder* variable declaration. We can use it for *y* as shown below:

```
# creating TensorFlow variables
y = tf.placeholder(tf.float32, [None, 1],
name='y')
```

Since we are not providing any initialization in the declaration, we should notify TensorFlow the data type of every element within the tensor. Our aim is to use *tf.float32*. Our second argument denotes the shape of the data to be injected in the variable. We need to use an array of size *(? x 1)*. Since we don't know the amount of data to supply to the array, we have used the "?". The placeholder is ready to accept *None* argument for the size declaration. After that, we are now able to inject any amount of 1-dimensional data we need into variable *y*.

Our program also expects a change in *ses.run(x,....)*. This is shown below:

```
x_out = ses.run(x, feed_dict={y: np.arange(0,
10)[:, np.newaxis]})
```

Note that the argument *feed_dict* has been added to the command *ses.run(x,...)*. We have removed the mystery and we have specified what the variable y is expected to be, which is 1-dimensional range between 0 and 10. As the argument name suggests, *feed_dict*, the input we are to supply is a Python dictionary, and every key will be the placeholder name that we are going to fill.

Now you are done and you have implemented a graph in TensorFlow. You should have the following code:

```
import tensorflow as tf
import numpy as np
# Begin by creating a TensorFlow constant
const = tf.constant(2.0, name="const")
# create the TensorFlow variables
y = tf.Variable(2.0, name='y')
z = tf.Variable(1.0, name='z')
# Let us create the operations
p = tf.add(y, z, name='p')
q = tf.add(z, const, name='q')
x = tf.multiply(p, q, name='x')
# creating a variable initialization
init_op = tf.global_variables_initializer()
# Launch the session
with tf.Session() as ses:
    # initialize the variables
    ses.run(init_op)
```

```
    # calculate the graph output
    x_out = ses.run(x)
    print("Variable x is {}".format(x_out))
# creating TensorFlow variables
y = tf.placeholder(tf.float32, [None, 1],
name='y')
x_out = ses.run(x, feed_dict={y: np.arange(0,
10)[:, np.newaxis]})
```

The code will return the following:

```
Variable x is 9.0
```

Here is another example that shows how to multiple two variables in TensorFlow fashion. The placeholder has been used together with a feed mechanism via the *run* method of the session:

```
import tensorflow as tf
a = tf.placeholder(tf.float32, name="a")
b = tf.placeholder(tf.float32, name="b")
c = tf.multiply(a, b, name="c")
with tf.Session() as ses:
    print ses.run(c, feed_dict={a: 2.1, b: 3.0})
```

The code will return the result given below:

```
6.3
```

Building Neural Networks

We will be demonstrating how you can a neural network with 3 layers in TensorFlow. We will use the MNIST dataset which serves as the "hello world" dataset for deep learning projects. This dataset is provided by the TensorFlow package. It has 28 /8 28 grayscale image all with handwritten digits. The dataset has 55,000 training rows, 5,000 validation rows and 10,000 testing rows.

The following lines of code can help us to load the dataset:

```
import tensorflow as tf
from tensorflow.examples.tutorials.mnist import
input_data
mnist = input_data.read_data_sets("MNIST_data/",
one_hot=True)
```

This returns the following:

```
Successfully downloaded train-images-idx3-ubyte.gz 9912422 bytes.
Extracting MNIST_data/train-images-idx3-ubyte.gz
Successfully downloaded train-labels-idx1-ubyte.gz 28881 bytes.
Extracting MNIST_data/train-labels-idx1-ubyte.gz
Successfully downloaded t10k-images-idx3-ubyte.gz 1648877 bytes.
Extracting MNIST_data/t10k-images-idx3-ubyte.gz
Successfully downloaded t10k-labels-idx1-ubyte.gz 4542 bytes.
Extracting MNIST_data/t10k-labels-idx1-ubyte.gz
```

The above output shows that the data has been imported successfully.

The argument *one_hot=True states that rather than the labels associated with every image being digit itself, that is, 4, it's a vector with a "one hot" node with the rest of the nodes being 0, that is,* [0, 0, 0, 0, 1, 0, 0, 0, 0, 0] . This makes it easy for one to load it into the output layer of their neural network.

We can create placeholder variables for our training data:

```
# Optimization variables
learning_rate = 0.5
epochs = 10
batch_size = 100
# Create placeholders for training data
# input a - for 28 x 28 pixels = 784
a = tf.placeholder(tf.float32, [None, 784])
# now create the placeholder for output data -
10 digits
b = tf.placeholder(tf.float32, [None, 10])
```

Note that the x input layer is 784 nodes corresponding to the $28 * 28$ pixels, which equals to 784. The "?" has been used to represent the unknown number of inputs that are to be used. The b output layer has 10 units which correspond 10 possible digits. Again, a has a size of $(? * 784)$, which represents an unknown number of inputs, marking the function of *placeholder* variable.

It is now time for us to set the bias and weight variables for our neural network. The number of weights/bias tensors always equals L-1, where L is the total number of layers. In our case, we will be setting up two tensors for each of them:

```
# we can declare the weights connecting our
input to hidden layer
W1 = tf.Variable(tf.random_normal([784, 300],
stddev=0.03), name='W1')
y1 = tf.Variable(tf.random_normal([300]),
name='y1')
# then the weights connecting hidden layer to
the output layer
W2 = tf.Variable(tf.random_normal([300, 10],
stddev=0.03), name='W2')
y2 = tf.Variable(tf.random_normal([10]),
name='y2')
y2 = tf.Variable(tf.random_normal([10]),
name='y2')
```

We began by declaring some variables, W1 and y1, representing the weights and the bias between the input and the hidden layer respectively. Our network should have 300 nodes in its hidden layer, so W1, which is the size for weight sensor will be [784, 300]. The values for the weights have been initialized using random normal distribution having a mean of 0 and a standard deviation of 0.03. We have also created the W2 and y2 variables to help in connecting the hidden layer of the network to the output layer.

Next, we should setup the node inputs and the activation functions for the nodes of the hidden layer. This is shown below:

```
# get the output of hidden layer
hidden_out = tf.add(tf.matmul(a, W1), y1)
hidden_out = tf.nn.relu(hidden_out)
```

In first line above, we have executed a matrix multiplication of weights (W1) by by input vector a then we added the bias *y1*. We used the *tf.matmul operation to run the multiplication of the matrix. The hidden_out operation has then been finalized by application of rectified linear unit activation to matrix multiplication then the bias. TensorFlow comes with a rectified linear unit activation that has readily been setup for us, which is named tf.nn.relu.*

We can now proceed to setup the output layer, which is y_:

```
b_ = tf.nn.softmax(tf.add(tf.matmul(hidden_out,
W2), y2))
```

We have again done the weight multiplication with the output obtained from the hidden layer (hidden_out) followed by addition of the bias, y2. The softmax activation has been used for the output layer, which comes included in TensorFlow and named *tf.nn.softmax*.

A cost or loss function must also be included for backpropagation/optimization to work on. The cross entropy function should be used for this case. The following TensorFlow code can help us implement the cross entropy function:

```
b_clipped = tf.clip_by_value(b_, 1e-10,
0.9999999)
cross_entropy = -tf.reduce_mean(tf.reduce_sum(b
* tf.log(b_clipped)+ (1 - b) * tf.log(1 -
b_clipped), axis=1))
```

The first line is an operation that helps us convert the output b_ to clipped version, which will be limited between 1e-10 and 0.999999.

This helps us avoid having `log(0)` during the operation when performing the training, which returns NaN and breaks the process of training. The second line above is simply a cross entropy calculation.

To perform the calculation, we use the *tf.reduce_sum* function provided by TensorFlow. The function takes the sum of the given axis for the tensor that you supply. In our case, the supplied tensor is element-wise cross-entropy calculation for a single node and training sample. The b and b_clipped are (m * 10) tensors. Hence we should get the first sum over the second axis. To specify this, we use the axis=1 argument, in which 1 denotes the second axis in cases where there is a system with zero-based indices in Python.

After that operation, we will have the *(m x 1)* tensor. To get the tensors' mean and complete the cross entropy cost calculation, we should call the *tf.reduce_mean* function of TensorFlow. The function will take the mean of any tensor that you provide. We now have a cost function that may be used for training purpose.

First, let us set the optimizer:

```
# Add the optimizer
optimizer =
tf.train.GradientDescentOptimizer(learning_rate=
learning_rate).minimize(cross_entropy)
```

We have used the gradient descent optimizer provided to us by TensorFlow. It should be initialized with the learning rate, hen defines what it should do, which is simply minimizing the cross entropy cost operation that we created. The function will, in turn, perform gradient descent and backpropagation on your behalf.

Before going to the main step, which involves running the operations, let us begin by setting up the variable initialization operation and an operation responsible for measuring the accuracy of the predictions. This can be done as shown below:

```
# Setting up the initialization operator
init_op = tf.global_variables_initializer()
# Creating the accuracy assessment operation
correct_prediction = tf.equal(tf.argmax(b, 1),
tf.argmax(b_, 1))
accuracy =
tf.reduce_mean(tf.cast(correct_prediction,
tf.float32))
```

The operation for a correct prediction, that is, *correct_prediction* makes use of *tf.equal* function provided by TensorFlow which returns True or False based on whether the arguments supplied to it are equal or not. The *tf.argmax* function usually returns the index of the maximum element in a tensor/vector. The *correct_prediction* operation will return a tensor sized (m * 1) of True and False values showing whether the neural network predicted the digit correctly. Our goal is to determine the accuracy of the mean from the tensor. We should begin by casting the type of *correct_prediction* operation from Boolean to TensorFlow float so as to perform the *reduce_mean* operation. After doing that, we will have the accuracy operation that can be used for the purpose of assessing the performance of the neural network.

Preparing for Training

We can now prepare for training of the neural network. The full code should be as follows:

```
# Launch the session
with tf.Session() as ses:
    # initializing the variables
    ses.run(init_op)
    total_batch = int(len(mnist.train.labels) /
batch_size)
    for epoch in range(epochs):
```

```
            avg_cost = 0
        for x in range(total_batch):
            batch_a, batch_b =
mnist.train.next_batch(batch_size=batch_size)
            _, z = ses.run([optimiser,
cross_entropy],
                        feed_dict={a: batch_a,
b: batch_b})
            avg_cost += b / total_batch
        print("Epoch:", (epoch + 1), "cost =",
"{:.3f}".format(avg_cost))
    print(ses.run(accuracy, feed_dict={x:
mnist.test.images, b: mnist.test.labels}))
```

The *"with"* operation has been setup and the initialization operation has been run. The third line is about the mini-batch training scheme that will be run for the neural network. In third line, we have calculated the number of batches that will be run for every epoch. We have then looped through every epoch then initialized the *avg_cost* variable to track the average cost entropy cost for every epoch. In the next line, we have extracted the randomized batch of samples, *batch_a* and *batch_b* from our training dataset. The MNIST dataset has a utility function named *next_batch*, that facilitates the extraction of batches of data for training.

In the next line, we are running two operations. The *ses.run* can take a list of operations and run them as its first argument. In such a case, when the *[optimiser, cross_entropy]* is supplied as the list, the two operations will be performed. This will give us two outputs, which will then be assigned to the variables _ and *z*. We are not much concerned about the output we get from the optimizer operation, but we are concerned about the output we get from the *cross_entropy* operation which was assigned to the variable *z*. The optimizer operation should be run on the batch samples. The *z* was then used for calculation of the average cost of the epoch.

We have then printed out the progress in average cost, then once done with training, the accuracy operation was execution to show the accuracy of the trained model on the test dataset.

You should now have the following code:

```
import tensorflow as tf
from tensorflow.examples.tutorials.mnist import
input_data
mnist = input_data.read_data_sets("MNIST_data/",
one_hot=True)
# Optimization variables
learning_rate = 0.5
epochs = 10
batch_size = 100
# Create placeholders for training data
# input a - for 28 x 28 pixels = 784
a = tf.placeholder(tf.float32, [None, 784])
# now create the placeholder for output data -
10 digits
b = tf.placeholder(tf.float32, [None, 10])
# we can declare the weights connecting our
input to hidden layer
W1 = tf.Variable(tf.random_normal([784, 300],
stddev=0.03), name='W1')
y1 = tf.Variable(tf.random_normal([300]),
name='y1')
# then the weights connecting hidden layer to
output layer
W2 = tf.Variable(tf.random_normal([300, 10],
stddev=0.03), name='W2')
y2 = tf.Variable(tf.random_normal([10]),
name='y2')
# get the output of hidden layer
hidden_out = tf.add(tf.matmul(a, W1), y1)
hidden_out = tf.nn.relu(hidden_out)
b_ = tf.nn.softmax(tf.add(tf.matmul(hidden_out,
W2), y2))
```

```python
b_clipped = tf.clip_by_value(b_, 1e-10,
0.9999999)
cross_entropy = -tf.reduce_mean(tf.reduce_sum(b
* tf.log(b_clipped)+ (1 - b) * tf.log(1 -
b_clipped), axis=1))
# Add the optimizer
optimizer =
tf.train.GradientDescentOptimizer(learning_rate=
learning_rate).minimize(cross_entropy)
# Setting up the initialization operator
init_op = tf.global_variables_initializer()
# Creating the accuracy assessment operation
correct_prediction = tf.equal(tf.argmax(b, 1),
tf.argmax(b_, 1))
accuracy =
tf.reduce_mean(tf.cast(correct_prediction,
tf.float32))
# Launch the session
with tf.Session() as ses:
    # initializing the variables
    ses.run(init_op)
    total_batch = int(len(mnist.train.labels) /
batch_size)
    for epoch in range(epochs):
        avg_cost = 0
        for x in range(total_batch):
            batch_a, batch_b =
mnist.train.next_batch(batch_size=batch_size)
            _, z = ses.run([optimiser,
cross_entropy],
                            feed_dict={a: batch_a,
b: batch_b})
            avg_cost += b / total_batch
        print("Epoch:", (epoch + 1), "cost =",
"{:.3f}".format(avg_cost))
    print(ses.run(accuracy, feed_dict={x:
mnist.test.images, b: mnist.test.labels}))
```

Chapter 11- Recurrent Neural Networks with TensorFlow

An artificial neural network has a simple structure and it all involves the multiplication of matrices. The inputs are first multiplied with random weights, and bias, and then passed through an activation function and the output values that are obtained are used for making predictions. This shows that this network is far from the reality.

The loss metric is applied. A higher loss function means a dumper model. To improve network knowledge, some optimization should be done by adjusting the weights. A method known as stochastic gradient descent is used to adjust the values of weights in the right direction. After the weights have been adjusted, the network is able to use a new batch of data to test new knowledge.

The error may be lower than what you had previously, but not small enough. The optimization process should be carried out iteratively until the error is minimized, that is, no more knowledge can be extracted.

However, there is a problem with this model in that it has no memory. This means that the input and output are independent. What this means is that the model doesn't care about what happened before. This raises a number of questions as when you need to predict sentences or time series since the network will need to have information about past words or historical data.

To solve this problem, a new architecture by the name Recurrent Neural Network (RNN) was developed.

In terms of structure, an RNN is the same as an ordinary neural network with the exception that it has some memory state added to the neurons. The computation for adding the memory is simple.

Consider a simple model having only one neuron that is fed by a batch of data. For the case of a traditional neural network, the model will produce the output by multiplying the input and the weight and the activation function. In an RNN, the output will be sent back to itself for a number of times. The *timestep* is the amount of time that the output becomes the input of the next matrix multiplication.

We need to code a simple RNN in TensorFlow. The network will be made up of the following:

- Four inputs
- Six neurons
- 2-time steps

This type of network is known as *recurrent* since it does a similar operation in every activate square. The network computes the weights of the inputs and the previous output then uses an activation function:

```
import tensorflow as tf
import numpy as np
n_inputs = 4
n_neurons = 6
n_timesteps = 2
#our data is a sequence of numbers, ranging
between 0 and 9 and put in 3 batches
X_batch = np.array([
        [[0, 2, 3, 5], [7, 8, 6, 4]], # First
batch
        [[3, 6, 5, 1], [0, 0, 0, 0]], # Second
batch
```

```
          [[6, 7, 8, 4], [6, 3, 4, 2]], # Third
batch
     ])
```

We can decide to build the network with a placeholder for our data, recurrent stage, and the output. Let us first define a placeholder for the data:

```
X = tf.placeholder(tf.float32, [None,
n_timesteps, n_inputs])
```

We have the following in the above definition:

- None- this is unknown and it will take the size of the batch.
- n_timesteps- this is the number of times that the network will send the output back to the neuron.
- n_inputs- this is the number of inputs for each batch.

We can no define the recurrent network. As we stated earlier, the network will have 6 neurons and it will compute a two dot product:

- The input data with the first set of weights that is 6 which is equal to the number of neurons.
- Previous output with the second set of weights that is 6 which correspond to the number of output.

In the first feed forward, the values of previous output will be equal to zeroes since there are no available values. To build an RNN, we use the *tf.contrib.rnn.BasicRNNCell* object. The argument to this object will be *num_units* which define the number of inputs. This is shown below:

```
basic_cell =
tf.contrib.rnn.BasicRNNCell(num_units=n_neurons)
```

Now that the network has been defined, we can compute the states and the outputs. This can be done as follows:

```
outputs, states = tf.nn.dynamic_rnn(basic_cell,
X, dtype=tf.float32)
```

The above object will use an internal loop to multiply the matrices for the right number of times.

What you should not forget is that the recurrent neuron is a function of all inputs of previous time steps. The network uses this to build its own memory. The information obtained from previous time can be propagated in future time. This is the magic of the RNN:

```
## Define the tensor shape
X = tf.placeholder(tf.float32, [None,
n_timesteps, n_inputs])
## Network definition
basic_cell =
tf.contrib.rnn.BasicRNNCell(num_units=n_neurons)
outputs, states = tf.nn.dynamic_rnn(basic_cell,
X, dtype=tf.float32)
init = tf.global_variables_initializer()
init = tf.global_variables_initializer()
with tf.Session() as sess:
    init.run()
    outputs_val = outputs.eval(feed_dict={X:
X_batch})
print(states.eval(feed_dict={X: X_batch}))
```

You print the values obtained from the previous state. The output that you get will be showing what you obtained from the previous state. You can now print the entire output, and you will realize that the results are previous output of every batch. This means that the previous output has the information regarding the whole sequence.

You just have to run the following print statements:

```
print(outputs_val)
print(outputs_val.shape)
```

The statements will return the following output:

```
[[[-0.99920565 -0.99989623 -0.8545807  -0.99602205 -0.99980509 -0.57997215]
  [-0.99999827 -0.99999988  0.99992251 -0.99878097 -0.99999934  0.99630177]]

 [[-0.99926811 -0.99986738  0.99891901 -0.99549693 -0.99998122  0.99612159]
  [ 0.56780976  0.23562071 -0.82923812  0.90174574  0.98718184 -0.84460682]]

 [[-0.99999559 -1.          0.99973011 -0.99998277 -1.          0.99809468]
  [-0.98698711 -0.99986392  0.97783029 -0.9296968  -0.94879383  0.72992796]]]
(3, 2, 6)
```

At the bottom of the above figure, it is clear that the output has a shape of (3, 2, 6) which means the following:

- 3: the total number of batches
- 2: the total number of the timestep
- 6: the total number of neurons

You can see that the process of optimizing a recurrent neural network is similar to the process of optimizing a traditional neural network.

RNNs are widely applied especially in predicting future events. They are widely used in business to predict the price of stocks and the direction that a market will take.

RNN in Time Series

RNN can be used with a time series data. Time series depend on previous time meaning that past values include very relevant information from which the network can learn. Time series prediction is used to estimate the future value of the series such as temperature, stock price, GDP etc.

117

It may be a bit tricky to prepare the values of a time series data. The goal is to predict the next value for a series, which means that the past information is very important as far as the prediction, is concerned. Consider the code given below:

```
import matplotlib.pyplot as plt
import matplotlib
import numpy as np
import pandas as pd
def create_ts(start = '2001', n = 201, freq =
'M'):
    rng = pd.date_range(start=start, periods=n,
freq=freq)
    a = pd.Series(np.random.uniform(-18, 18,
size=len(rng)), rng).cumsum()
    return a
a= create_ts(start = '2001', n = 222, freq =
'M')
print(a.tail(5))
```

We have created a function to return a dataset with random values for every day between the specified periods of time. The last 5 values of the output are as follows:

```
2019-02-28    259.470036
2019-03-31    261.466766
2019-04-30    272.602929
2019-05-31    285.974806
2019-06-30    271.006378
Freq: M, dtype: float64
((201,), (21,))
```

Let us create a plot from the data:

```
a = create_ts(start = '2001', n = 222)
#On the Left Side
plt.figure(figsize=(11,4))
```

118

```
plt.subplot(121)
plt.plot(a.index, a)
plt.plot(a.index[90:100], a[90:100], "b-",
linewidth=3, label="Training instance")
plt.title("A time series (generated)",
fontsize=14)
#On the Right Side
plt.subplot(122)
plt.title("Training instance", fontsize=14)
plt.plot(a.index[90:100], a[90:100], "b-",
markersize=8, label="instance")
plt.plot(a.index[91:101], a[91:101], "bo",
markersize=10, label="target",
markerfacecolor='red')
plt.legend(loc="upper left")
plt.xlabel("Time")
plt.show()
```

On the right part of the graph, you should see all the series.

Predictions with RNN

We can build an RNN to predict the series that we have above. We should first define hyper parameters for the model including the following:

- The number of inputs: 1
- The time step: 10
- The number of neurons: 120
- The number of outputs: 1

We need the network to learn from a sequence of 10 days and have 120 recurrent neurons. The model should be fed with one input, that is, one day. You can change the values if you need to see whether the model made an improvement or not.

As usual, before training the model, we should split the dataset into training and test sets. Since the entire dataset has 222 points, let us use the first 201 of them as the training set and the last 21 data points as the test set.

Once the splitting is done successfully, we should then create a model with the batches. In the batches, you will have both X and Y values. The X values will be lagged by one period. This means you should use the first 200 observations and the time step will be 10. The X_batches object should have 20 batches sized 10*1. The y_batches should have the same shape as X_batches object. However, it should have one period ahead.

Splitting the Dataset

We should first split the dataset into training and test sets. Let us convert the series into a numpy array then we define the windows (the times the network should learn from), the number of the input, output and size of train set:

```
series = np.array(a)
n_windows = 20
n_input =  1
n_output = 1
size_train = 171
```

After the above definitions, we can split the dataset as follows:

```
## Split the dataset
train = series[:size_train]
test = series[size_train:]
print(train.shape, test.shape)
```

The above print statement returns the following:

```
## Split the dataset
train = series[:size_train]
test = series[size_train:]
print(train.shape, test.shape)
```

The above print statement should return the following:

```
((201,), (21,))
```

At this point, you should have the following code to make sure you are progressing the right way:

```python
import matplotlib.pyplot as plt
import matplotlib
import numpy as np
import pandas as pd
def create_ts(start = '2001', n = 201, freq =
'M'):
    rng = pd.date_range(start=start, periods=n,
freq=freq)
    a = pd.Series(np.random.uniform(-18, 18,
size=len(rng)), rng).cumsum()
    return a
a= create_ts(start = '2001', n = 222, freq =
'M')
#print(a.tail(5))
series = np.array(a)
n_windows = 20
n_input =  1
n_output = 1
size_train = 171
## Split the dataset
train = series[:size_train]
test = series[size_train:]
print(train.shape, test.shape)
```

We should now create a function that will return X_batches and y_batches.

We should write a function that will create the batches. X batches are lagged by only one period, so we take a value of t-1. The output from the function should be in three dimensions. The first dimensions

121

should be equal to the number of batches; the second should be of window size while the last one should be the number of the input.

It is tricky for one to choose the data points correctly. For X data points, choose observations from t=1 up to t=200. For the y data point, return observations from t=2 up to t=201. After getting the correct data points, it will be easy for you to reshape the series.

For an object with the batches to be constructed, the dataset should be split into 10 batches all having an equal length, that is, 20. The reshape method can be used then parameters of -1 pass for the series to be the same as the batch size. 20 denote the number of observations for each batch while 1 denotes the number of the input. If you need a forecast of two days, then change the data by 2:

```
x_data = train[:size_train-1]: #Chooset all
training instance less one day
X_batches = x_data.reshape(-1, windows, input):
#create right shape for batch
def create_batches(df, windows, input, output):
    ## Creating X
        x_data = train[:size_train-1] # Choose
the data
        X_batches = x_data.reshape(-1, windows,
input)   # Reshaping the data
    ## Creating y
        y_data = train[n_output:size_train]
        y_batches = y_data.reshape(-1, windows,
output)
        return X_batches, y_batches
```

Now that we have defined the function, let us call it to create the batches:

```
X_batches, y_batches = create_batches(df =
train,
                              windows =
n_windows,
```

```
                                        input =
n_input,
                                        output =
n_output)
```

At this point, you can print the shape to be sure that you have the right dimensions:

```
((10, 20, 1), (10, 20, 1))
```

We should create a test set with one batch of data only and 20 observations. Note that you should forecast the days after days. This means that the value that is predicted second will depend on the true value of the first day of test dataset. In fact, you will be able to know the true value.

```
X_test, y_test = create_batches(df = test,
windows = 20, input = 1, output = 1)
print(X_test.shape, y_test.shape)
```

This will return the same shape as shown below:

```
((10, 20, 1), (10, 20, 1))
```

Building the Model

For you to build the model, you should define the following three parts:

1. The variable with tensors
2. RNN
3. The loss and optimization

Variables

The X and y variables should be specified with the right shape. This is a trivial step. The tensor has a similar dimension as objects X_batches and y_batches.

The tensor X for instance is a placeholder with three dimensions:

- None: size of the batch
- n_windows: Length of windows. That is, the number of times your model looks backward
- n_input: the number of input

The result of this is shown below:

```
tf.placeholder(tf.float32, [None, n_windows, n_input])
```

Here is the code for constructing the tensors:

```
X = tf.placeholder(tf.float32, [None, n_windows, n_input])
y = tf.placeholder(tf.float32, [None, n_windows, n_output])
```

Creating the RNN

It is now time for us to define the architecture of the network. This should be done using the *BasicRNNCell* and *dynamic_rnn* objects from the TensorFlow estimator. This can be done as shown below:

```
basic_cell =
tf.contrib.rnn.BasicRNNCell(num_units=r_neuron,
activation=tf.nn.relu)
rnn_output, states =
tf.nn.dynamic_rnn(basic_cell, X,
dtype=tf.float32)
```

The next part will create an easier computation for us. The run output should be transformed to a dense layer then converted to have similar dimension as the input. This is shown below:

```
stacked_rnn_output = tf.reshape(rnn_output, [-1,
r_neuron])
stacked_outputs =
tf.layers.dense(stacked_rnn_output, n_output)
outputs = tf.reshape(stacked_outputs, [-1,
n_windows, n_output])
```

Creating the Loss and Optimization

The optimization of the model is determined by the task that you are performing. In this case, we are making a prediction on a continuous variable. In continuous variables, the goal of performing optimization is to reduce the mean square error. In TensorFlow, such metrics are constructed using the following:

```
tf.reduce_sum(tf.square(outputs - y))
```

The rest of the code is the same as before, hence the loss can be minimized using the Adam optimizer as shown below:

```
tf.train.AdamOptimizer(learning_rate=learning_ra
te)
optimizer.minimize(loss)
```

Let us now pack everything together and prepare the model for training:

```
tf.reset_default_graph()
r_neuron = 120
X = tf.placeholder(tf.float32, [None, n_windows,
n_input])
y = tf.placeholder(tf.float32, [None, n_windows,
n_output])
```

```
basic_cell =
tf.contrib.rnn.BasicRNNCell(num_units=r_neuron,
activation=tf.nn.relu)
rnn_output, states =
tf.nn.dynamic_rnn(basic_cell, X,
dtype=tf.float32)
stacked_rnn_output = tf.reshape(rnn_output, [-1,
r_neuron])
stacked_outputs =
tf.layers.dense(stacked_rnn_output, n_output)
outputs = tf.reshape(stacked_outputs, [-1,
n_windows, n_output])
## Loss and optimization
learning_rate = 0.001
loss = tf.reduce_sum(tf.square(outputs - y))
optimizer =
tf.train.AdamOptimizer(learning_rate=learning_ra
te)
training_op = optimizer.minimize(loss)
init = tf.global_variables_initializer()
```

We need to train our model for 1500 epochs and print the loss after every 150 iterations. Once the model has been trained, we will evaluate it using the test data set then create an object having the predictions. This can be done as shown below:

```
iteration = 1500
with tf.Session() as sess:
    init.run()
    for iters in range(iteration):
        sess.run(training_op, feed_dict={X:
X_batches, y: y_batches})
        if iters % 150 == 0:
            mse = loss.eval(feed_dict={X:
X_batches, y: y_batches})
            print(iters, "\tMSE:", mse)
    y_pred = sess.run(outputs, feed_dict={X:
X_test})
```

At this point, you should have the following code:

```python
import matplotlib.pyplot as plt
import matplotlib
import numpy as np
import pandas as pd
import tensorflow as tf
def create_ts(start = '2001', n = 201, freq =
'M'):
    rng = pd.date_range(start=start, periods=n,
freq=freq)
    a = pd.Series(np.random.uniform(-18, 18,
size=len(rng)), rng).cumsum()
    return a
a= create_ts(start = '2001', n = 222, freq =
'M')
#print(a.tail(5))
series = np.array(a)
n_windows = 20
n_input =  1
n_output = 1
size_train = 201
## Split the dataset
train = series[:size_train]
test = series[size_train:]
#print(train.shape, test.shape)
x_data = train[:size_train-1]
X_batches = x_data.reshape(-1, n_windows,
n_input) #create right shape for batch
def create_batches(df, windows, input, output):
    ## Creating X
        x_data = train[:size_train-1] # Choose
the data
        X_batches = x_data.reshape(-1, windows,
input)  # Reshaping the data
    ## Creating y
        y_data = train[n_output:size_train]
        y_batches = y_data.reshape(-1,
n_windows, output)
        return X_batches, y_batches
      X_batches, y_batches = create_batches(df =
train,
```

127

```
                                      windows =
n_windows,
                                        input =
n_input,
                                       output =
n_output)
#print(X_batches.shape, y_batches.shape)

X_test, y_test = create_batches(df = test,
windows = 20,input = 1, output = 1)
#print(X_test.shape, y_test.shape)
tf.placeholder(tf.float32, [None, n_windows,
n_input])
tf.reset_default_graph()
r_neuron = 120
X = tf.placeholder(tf.float32, [None, n_windows,
n_input])
y = tf.placeholder(tf.float32, [None, n_windows,
n_output])
basic_cell =
tf.contrib.rnn.BasicRNNCell(num_units=r_neuron,
activation=tf.nn.relu)
rnn_output, states =
tf.nn.dynamic_rnn(basic_cell, X,
dtype=tf.float32)
stacked_rnn_output = tf.reshape(rnn_output, [-1,
r_neuron])
stacked_outputs =
tf.layers.dense(stacked_rnn_output, n_output)
outputs = tf.reshape(stacked_outputs, [-1,
n_windows, n_output])
## Loss and optimization
learning_rate = 0.001
loss = tf.reduce_sum(tf.square(outputs - y))
optimizer =
tf.train.AdamOptimizer(learning_rate=learning_ra
te)
training_op = optimizer.minimize(loss)
init = tf.global_variables_initializer()
iteration = 1500
```

128

```
with tf.Session() as sess:
    init.run()
    for iters in range(iteration):
        sess.run(training_op, feed_dict={X:
X_batches, y: y_batches})
        if iters % 150 == 0:
            mse = loss.eval(feed_dict={X:
X_batches, y: y_batches})
            print(iters, "\tMSE:", mse)
    y_pred = sess.run(outputs, feed_dict={X:
X_test})
```

The code should give you the following result once executed:

```
(0, '\tMSE:', 855708.38)
(150, '\tMSE:', 14078.414)
(300, '\tMSE:', 3596.8198)
(450, '\tMSE:', 2530.5332)
(600, '\tMSE:', 1972.0417)
(750, '\tMSE:', 1601.2076)
(900, '\tMSE:', 1394.1292)
(1050, '\tMSE:', 1305.7087)
(1200, '\tMSE:', 1184.1237)
(1350, '\tMSE:', 1065.718)
```

You are now able to plot the actual value of the series with predicted value. Once the model has been corrected, the predicted values should be added to the top of actual values.

It is very clear that the model has a room for improvement. It is your role to change the values of hyper parameters like window and batch size of number of recurrent neurons. Here is how to create a plot of the Predicted vs. the Actual values:

```
plt.title("Predicted vs Actual", fontsize=14)
```

```
plt.plot(pd.Series(np.ravel(y_test)), "bo",
markersize=8, label="Actual", color='green')
plt.plot(pd.Series(np.ravel(y_pred)), "r.",
markersize=8, label="Forecast", color='red')
plt.legend(loc="lower left")
plt.xlabel("Time")
plt.show()
```

You are done. A recurrent neural network is an architecture for dealing with text and time series analysis. The output from the previous state is fed back to fed back to help preserve the network memory over time or a sequence of words.

Chapter 12- Linear Classifier

In supervised learning, the most popular tasks are the linear regression and linear classifier. Linear regression works by predicting a value while linear classifier works by predicting a class. We will be focusing on a linear classifier.

Classification tasks form 80% of machine learning tasks. The aim of classification is to predict the probability of every class when you are given a set of inputs. The label is usually a discrete value known as a *class*.

If the label is made up of two classes only, the learning algorithm is referred to as a *binary classifier*. If the label has more than two classifiers, it is known as a multiclass classifier.

We will be using a census dataset to implement a linear classifier in TensorFlow. We need to use the variables in the dataset to predict the level of income. The income is a binary variable:

- A value of 1 if income > 50k
- 0 if the income < 50k.

This means the income will be the label.

Here are the 8 categorical variables for the dataset:

- workplace
- education
- marital
- occupation
- relationship
- race

- sex
- native_country

Here are six continuous variables for the dataset:

- age
- fnlwgt
- education_num
- capital_gain
- capital_loss
- hours_week

You will learn how to train a linear classifier in TensorFlow estimator and improve its accuracy metric. Let us start:

Importing the Data

Let us begin by importing the libraries that are needed:

```
import tensorflow as tf
import pandas as pd
```

We need to import the data from the UCI repository then define its column names:

```
## Defining the path data
COLUMNS = ['age','workclass', 'fnlwgt',
'education', 'education_num', 'marital',
          'occupation', 'relationship', 'race',
'sex', 'capital_gain', 'capital_loss',
          'hours_week', 'native_country',
'label']
PATH = "https://archive.ics.uci.edu/ml/machine-
learning-databases/adult/adult.data"
PATH_test =
"https://archive.ics.uci.edu/ml/machine-
learning-databases/adult/adult.test"
```

Data kept online is already split into train and test sets. You can view these sets as follows:

```
train_set = pd.read_csv(PATH,
skipinitialspace=True, names = COLUMNS,
index_col=False)
test_set = pd.read_csv(PATH_test,skiprows = 1,
skipinitialspace=True, names = COLUMNS,
index_col=False)
print(train_set)
print(test_set)
```

It returns the following:

	age	workclass	fnlwgt	education	education_num
0	39	State-gov	77516	Bachelors	13
1	50	Self-emp-not-inc	83311	Bachelors	13
2	38	Private	215646	HS-grad	9
3	53	Private	234721	11th	7
4	28	Private	338409	Bachelors	13
5	37	Private	284582	Masters	14
6	49	Private	160187	9th	5
7	52	Self-emp-not-inc	209642	HS-grad	9
8	31	Private	45781	Masters	14
9	42	Private	159449	Bachelors	13

Above is just a section of the data as the data is long.

TensorFlow needs a Boolean value to train the classifier. This means the values should be cast from a string to an integer. The label is now an object, but it should be transformed into a numeric value. Let us create a dictionary:

```
label = {'<=50K': 0,'>50K': 1}
train_set.label = [label[item] for item in
train_set.label]
label_t = {'<=50K.': 0,'>50K.': 1}
test_set.label = [label_t[item] for item in
test_set.label]
```

The train data set has 24,720 incomes that are lower than 50K and 7841 that are above. This is almost similar for the test set:

```
print(train_set["label"].value_counts())
print(test_set["label"].value_counts())
print(train_set.dtypes)
```

Here is a section of output from the above code:

```
0      24720
1       7841
Name: label, dtype: int64
0      12435
1       3846
Name: label, dtype: int64
age                    int64
workclass             object
fnlwgt                 int64
education             object
```

Data Preparation

Before training the model, we should prepare the features that are to be included into it. The estimator requires a list of features that are needed to train the model. The column data should be converted into a tensor.

We can define two lists of features depending on their type then pass them to *feature_columns* of the estimator:

```
## Adding features
### Defining the continuous list
CONT_FEATURES = ['age',
'fnlwgt','capital_gain', 'education_num',
'capital_loss', 'hours_week']
### Defining the categorical list
```

```
CATEG_FEATURES = ['workclass', 'education',
'marital', 'occupation', 'relationship', 'race',
'sex', 'native_country']
```

The following code will allow you to see what is happening behind the *feature_column.numeric_column*. We will print the converted value for the *age* to help you understand:

```
def show_transformation(feature = "age",
continuous = True, size = 2):
    #X = fc.numeric_column(feature)
    ## Creating the feature name
    feature_names = [
    feature]
    ## Creating a dictionary with the data
    d = dict(zip(feature_names,
[train_set[feature]]))
    ## Converting age
    if continuous == True:
        cont =
tf.feature_column.numeric_column(feature)
        feature_columns = [cont]
    else:
        cont =
tf.feature_column.categorical_column_with_hash_b
ucket(feature, hash_bucket_size=size)
        c_indicator =
tf.feature_column.indicator_column(cont)
        feature_columns = [c_indicator]
## print the value
    input_layer = tf.feature_column.input_layer(
        features=d,
        feature_columns=feature_columns
        )
    ## Creating a lookup table
    zero = tf.constant(0, dtype=tf.float32)
    where = tf.not_equal(input_layer, zero)
    ## Return the lookup tble
    indices = tf.where(where)
    values = tf.gather_nd(input_layer, indices)
```

```
   ## Initiating a graph
   sess = tf.Session()
   ## Print the value
   print(sess.run(input_layer))
show_transformation(feature = "age", continuous
= True)
```

Here is a section of output from the code:

```
hours_week              int64
native_country         object
label                   int64
dtype: object
[[ 39.]
 [ 50.]
 [ 38.]
 ...,
 [ 58.]
 [ 22.]
 [ 52.]]
```

The values are similar to what we have in *train_set*.

```
continuous_features =
[tf.feature_column.numeric_column(k) for k in
CONTI_FEATURES]
```

Categorical ways can be converted through a number of ways. Consider thie for the sex column:

```
show_transformation(feature = "sex", continuous
= False, size = 2)
```

Then add this code:

```
relationship =
tf.feature_column.categorical_column_with_vocabu
lary_list(
```

```
'relationship', [
    'Husband', 'Not-in-family', 'Wife',
'Own-child', 'Unmarried',
    'Other-relative'])
```

Here is the code to help you in printing the encoding. The fastest way of transforming data is by using the *categorical_column_with_hash_bucket* method. This methods only expects you to specify the number of columns as well as the key column. The number of specified buckets will form the maximum amount of groups that TensorFlow will be able to create.

Let us create a loop over all categorical features:

```
categorical_features =
[tf.feature_column.categorical_column_with_hash_
bucket(k, hash_bucket_size=1000) for k in
CATEG_FEATURES]
```

Training the Classifier

TensorFlow has an estimator for Linear Regression and Linear Classification:

- Linear regression: LinearRegressor
- Linear classification: LinearClassifier

Since this is a Linear Classifier, we can have the following in our code:

```
model = tf.estimator.LinearClassifier(
    n_classes = 2,
    model_dir="ongoing/train",
    feature_columns=categorical_features+
continuous_features)
```

Now that the classifier has been defined, it is time for us to create the input function. We will use a batch of size 128 then shuffle the data.

```
FEATURES = ['age','workclass', 'fnlwgt',
'education', 'education_num', 'marital',
'occupation', 'relationship', 'race', 'sex',
'capital_gain', 'capital_loss', 'hours_week',
'native_country']
LABEL= 'label'
def get_input_fn(data_set, num_epochs=None,
n_batch = 128, shuffle=True):
    return tf.estimator.inputs.pandas_input_fn(
        x=pd.DataFrame({k: data_set[k].values for
k in FEATURES}),
        y = pd.Series(data_set[LABEL].values),
        batch_size=n_batch,
        num_epochs=num_epochs,
        shuffle=shuffle)
```

We have created a function with the arguments that are needed by the linear estimator, that is, number of epochs, the number of batches then shuffle the dataset or note.

We need to train the model via the *model. train* object. We will use a function that was defined previously to pass correct data to the model. The batch size has been set to 128 while the number of epochs has been set to None. The model will be trained in over 1000 steps:

```
model.train(input_fn=get_input_fn(df_train,

num_epochs=None,

                                  n_batch =
128,

shuffle=False),

steps=1000)
```

You will realize that the loss has decreased in the last few steps of training the model.

The model can be evaluated using the test data set and see well it performed. The evaluate object can be used for evaluation of the performance of the model. The model should be fed with the test data then the number of epochs set to 1, that is, to allow the data to get into the model only one time.

```
model.evaluate(input_fn=get_input_fn(test_set,

num_epochs=1,
                                          n_batch =
128,

shuffle=False),

steps=1000)
```

All the metrics will be returned by TensorFlow. We have an unbalanced label, hence you should get a high accuracy.

At this point, you should have the following code:

```
import tensorflow as tf
import pandas as pd
## Defining the path data
COLUMNS = ['age','workclass', 'fnlwgt',
'education', 'education_num', 'marital',
          'occupation', 'relationship', 'race',
'sex', 'capital_gain', 'capital_loss',
          'hours_week', 'native_country',
'label']
PATH = "https://archive.ics.uci.edu/ml/machine-
learning-databases/adult/adult.data"
PATH_test =
"https://archive.ics.uci.edu/ml/machine-
learning-databases/adult/adult.test"
train_set = pd.read_csv(PATH,
skipinitialspace=True, names = COLUMNS,
index_col=False)
```

```python
test_set = pd.read_csv(PATH_test,skiprows = 1,
skipinitialspace=True, names = COLUMNS,
index_col=False)
#print(train_set)
#print(test_set)
label = {'<=50K': 0,'>50K': 1}
train_set.label = [label[item] for item in
train_set.label]
label_t = {'<=50K.': 0,'>50K.': 1}
test_set.label = [label_t[item] for item in
test_set.label]
print(train_set["label"].value_counts())
print(test_set["label"].value_counts())
print(train_set.dtypes)
## Adding features
### Defining the continuous list
CONT_FEATURES  = ['age',
'fnlwgt','capital_gain', 'education_num',
'capital_loss', 'hours_week']
### Defining the categorical list
CATEG_FEATURES = ['workclass', 'education',
'marital', 'occupation', 'relationship', 'race',
'sex', 'native_country']
def show_transformation(feature = "age",
continuous = True, size = 2):
    #X = fc.numeric_column(feature)
    ## Creating the feature name
    feature_names = [
    feature]
    ## Creating a dictionary with the data
    d = dict(zip(feature_names,
[train_set[feature]]))
    ## Converting age
    if continuous == True:
        cont =
tf.feature_column.numeric_column(feature)
        feature_columns = [cont]
    else:
```

```python
        cont =
tf.feature_column.categorical_column_with_hash_b
ucket(feature, hash_bucket_size=size)
        c_indicator =
tf.feature_column.indicator_column(cont)
        feature_columns = [c_indicator]
## print the value
    input_layer = tf.feature_column.input_layer(
        features=d,
        feature_columns=feature_columns
        )
    ## Creating a lookup table
    zero = tf.constant(0, dtype=tf.float32)
    where = tf.not_equal(input_layer, zero)
    ## Return the lookup tble
    indices = tf.where(where)
    values = tf.gather_nd(input_layer, indices)
    ## Initiating a graph
    sess = tf.Session()
    ## Print the value
    print(sess.run(input_layer))
#show_transformation(feature = "age", continuous
= True)
continuous_features =
[tf.feature_column.numeric_column(k) for k in
CONT_FEATURES]
show_transformation(feature = "sex", continuous
= False, size = 2)
relationship =
tf.feature_column.categorical_column_with_vocabu
lary_list(
    'relationship', [
        'Husband', 'Not-in-family', 'Wife',
'Own-child', 'Unmarried',
        'Other-relative'])
categorical_features =
[tf.feature_column.categorical_column_with_hash_
bucket(k, hash_bucket_size=1000) for k in
CATEG_FEATURES]
model = tf.estimator.LinearClassifier(
```

```python
    n_classes = 2,
    model_dir="ongoing/train",
    feature_columns=categorical_features+
continuous_features)
print(model)

FEATURES = ['age','workclass', 'fnlwgt',
'education', 'education_num', 'marital',
'occupation', 'relationship', 'race', 'sex',
'capital_gain', 'capital_loss', 'hours_week',
'native_country']
LABEL= 'label'
def get_input_fn(data_set, num_epochs=None,
n_batch = 128, shuffle=True):
    return tf.estimator.inputs.pandas_input_fn(
        x=pd.DataFrame({k: data_set[k].values for
k in FEATURES}),
        y = pd.Series(data_set[LABEL].values),
        batch_size=n_batch,
        num_epochs=num_epochs,
        shuffle=shuffle)
model.train(input_fn=get_input_fn(df_train,

num_epochs=None,
                                  n_batch =
128,

shuffle=False),

steps=1000)
model.evaluate(input_fn=get_input_fn(test_set,

num_epochs=1,
                                  n_batch =
128,

shuffle=False),

steps=1000)
```

Conclusion

Machine learning is a branch of artificial intelligence that involves the design and development of systems capable of showing an improvement in performance based on their previous experiences. This means that when reacting to the same situation, a machine should show an improvement from time to time. With machine learning, software systems are able to predict accurately without having to be programmed explicitly. The goal of machine learning is to build algorithms which can receive input data then use statistical analysis so as to predict the output value in an acceptable range.

Machine learning originated from pattern recognition and the theory that computers are able to learn without the need for programming them to perform tasks. Researchers in the field of artificial intelligence wanted to determine whether computers are able to learn from data. Machine learning is an iterative approach, and this is why models are able to adapt as they are being exposed to new data. Models learn from their previous computations so as to give repeatable, reliable results and decisions.

17339418R00085

Printed in Great Britain
by Amazon